Contents

A
STRAIGHTFORWARD
GUIDE
TO
BUYING AND SELLING
PROPERTY AT AUCTION

ROGER SPROSTON

Straightforward Guides

978-1-84716-477-3

Printed by Grosvenor Press London

Cover design by Bookworks Islington

Whilst every effort has been made to ensure that the information contained within this book is correct at the time of going to press, the author and publisher can take no responsibility for the errors or omissions contained within.

Introduction

Most of us have watched programmes on television such as 'Homes Under the Hammer'. This involves people, mainly investors, purchasing a property at auction and refurbishing it and selling it on. However, there are also many non-investors looking to buy a property at a decent price and live in it as their main home. This book is intended for both of the above groups. It also covers the large variety of other properties that come up for auction, including commercial properties.

In addition to providing advice and information for buyers of property, we also offer advice for the seller, explaining how the auction process works.

For those buying a residential property at auction, both buy-to-let investors and those looking to purchase a home, auctions can mean that buying a house doesn't involve endless viewings with estate agents and then months of waiting to exchange contracts, with the possibility of gazumping along the way. Once you have made your bid and the gavel comes down then the property is yours on the spot.

Buying a house, particularly in the distorted London housing market, can now be an extremely frustrating and uncertain process. This is why buyers are now looking to auctions to circumvent the hassle of looking for, or selling, a house.

With house prices continuing to rise, people are looking for value, looking for some way to get onto the property ladder and are turning to auctions, where there are still bargains to be found and the usual rules relating to house purchase do not apply.

There has been a big year-on-year rise in the auctions side of the residential property market. Properties at auction can sell at a discount because of the seller's circumstances, for example bankruptcy, repossession or the need to clear debts. There is also a lot of ex-council stock, and some private sellers simply like the speed and simplicity of the process.

Needless to say, there are many things to watch out for and many pitfalls to avoid when buying property at auction. These will be discussed in depth in this book. In short, when buying at auction:

- be certain of what you want and what you want to do with it
- Never rely on the catalogue alone-always go to see the property.
- If possible, get a surveyor involved before making a bid for the property-this will save you a lot of time and money later on
- Talk to the auctioneer in advance of the sale-they are duty bound to let you know of any problems that they know of
- Make sure that you understand the legal pack and have a firm idea of what you are letting yourself in for
- Make sure that you have the finance in place
- make sure that you understand the process-try to attend an auction before you put in your own bids.

This book should prove invaluable in taking you through the process of buying (and selling) property at auction and put you in a strong position when bidding. Remember, as we have stated above, when the gavel falls the property is yours-make sure that you have bought the right one and are on safe ground.

Chapter 1

How Auctions Work

Whilst most of us have a basic idea of how auctions work, and have watched various programmes which deal with property and other lots, it is important to delve a little deeper and gain a broad understanding of what an auction is, specifically a property auction, what can be bought and sold at property auctions and how we can close deals and get what we want on the day.

The below is a general overview of how an auction works and what actually happens on the day. It offers advice to both buyers and sellers. We will be discussing each area in detail in the following chapters. However, this will give you a general flavour of the whole process.

What is a property auction?
The process is very similar to the normal method of private sale. However, for an auction sale the seller and their solicitor carry out all the necessary paperwork and legal investigations prior to the auction. Subject to the property receiving an acceptable bid,

the property will be 'sold' on auction day with a legally binding exchange of contracts and a fixed completion date.

Different types of property auction houses

Auction houses vary in size and the amount of business that they conduct and the frequency with which they hold auctions. Most will sell both residential and commercial property and each will have its own style of operation, and fee structure.

Large auction houses will hold auctions frequently, perhaps every two months and will have around 250 lots for sale. A lot of the auctions happen in London but will also be held nearer to home. Therefore, a large estate agent which has its main base in the Midlands, and also holds auctions, will tend to have them in Birmingham, Derby, and in the case of the auction we attended, featured in the final chapter, in Nottingham.

Most of the large auction houses will deal with property put forward by large institutions, such as banks selling repossessions and also local authorities and will advertise the sales in the mainstream media and trade papers.

The medium size auction houses will hold auctions as frequently as they can, in regional venues, such as racecourses and conference centres, and depending on stock, usually every two to three months, tending to advertise locally.

The small auction houses will have far fewer lots and will hold their sales in smaller local venues. They may advertise in local press but more often will trade on word of mouth.

Those who attend auctions

As you might imagine, all sorts of people attend auctions. The common denominator is that they are all interested in buying property.

Property investors are most common at auction, people who are starting out building a portfolio or those who have large portfolios that they wish to expand. They tend to fall into two groups, those who are after capital appreciation, i.e. buy at a low value and build the capital value and those who are looking for rental income. Then there are the property traders who like a quick profit from buying and 'flipping' property. These types usually have intimate knowledge of an area and are well placed to make a quick profit.

Then we have the developers who look for small profitable sites or larger sites where property can be built and sold on. The sites can have existing buildings on them or can be vacant lots with or without planning permission. Last, but not least, we have those people who intend to buy solely for the purpose of owner occupation, look to buy a below- value property that they can redesign and make their own.

What types of property are suitable for auction?
There is strong demand for all types of properties offered at auction. These may be properties requiring updating, those with short leases, development sites with or without planning permission, repossessions, forced sales, investment properties, ground rents, probates, receivership sales and local authority properties. However, any type of property can be sold at auction and initially the property will be inspected to discuss specific criteria and the current situation. Extensive research will be carried out by the auction house and advice offered as to whether auction is the appropriate method of sale. The below represents a cross section of what might be found at auction.

Properties for Improvement
Properties in need of updating make ideal auction Lots. They are in great demand from refurbishment specialists and private buyers, keen to undertake a project for their own occupation or

for resale. They also appeal to buy-to-let investors who carry out the improvements then retain them as part of a property portfolio.

Tenanted Properties

Residential houses and flats with tenants in residence sell well at auction. Notice doesn't need to be served notice on tenants, and rental income continues to be received right up to completion.

Residential Investments

Houses in multiple occupation and blocks of flats are sold at auction as valuable investments. Here it is the rent level that determines the sale price, just as much as the building itself.

Development Propositions

Derelict or disused farm buildings, empty commercial premises, buildings with potential for conversion or change of use, can all sell well at auction. In some locations a change to residential can significantly add to the value of a property, in other situations there may be space for additional dwellings or to substantially enlarge the property.

Building Land

There is no better way of ensuring a seller achieves best price for a building plot or parcel of development land than to offer it for sale by auction. Builders will be able to consult with architects, planners etc., and be ready to bid in the auction room.

Mixed Use Properties

Properties that have twin uses or a variety of potential future uses are ideal for sale by auction. Retail shops with accommodation above appeal to investors as well as owner-occupiers. Further conversion work can often be undertaken and the property tailored to suit the purchaser's special requirements.

Commercial Investments

Retail shops, offices, industrial units, garage blocks and parking areas - an ever increasing number of commercial investments are being sold at auction. It doesn't matter whether they are vacant or tenanted, with lease renewal soon needed or with a long way to run.

Unique Properties

There are always some rare entries, sought after property and prime locations that need to be sold in a competitive bidding environment. Unexpectedly high prices have been achieved by this route.

Amenity Land and Other Property

Paddocks, meadows, fields, moorings, amenity land and also other unusual land parcels are all sold at auction. If it is property or land that is surplus to requirements, the likelihood is a buyer can be found at auction. If it has a value, and is worth marketing, it is worth considering a disposal by auction.

What is the timeframe for an auction sale and what happens next?

The latest date for entering property for an auction is usually five to six weeks prior to the auction. Once the marketing agreement has been signed, the property will be placed in the catalogue and a board erected. Each seller's legal representative will be contacted to obtain a legal pack, which the seller must produce. This pack should generally include office copy entries and plans, the local search, leases (if applicable) and any other relevant documents. All properties at auction are sold under the General Conditions of Sale and, with the legal pack, also require any Special Conditions of Sale to be attached. These are matters that are relevant solely to the lot being sold. The marketing period starts five to six weeks before a sale. The details of all the lots to be offered in the next sale, including colour photographs of each property, viewing arrangements and any other relevant information will then be published. A few days prior to the auction, the reserve price will be agreed.

What happens on the day?
The lots will be offered and the bidding taken to the highest possible level and once the gavel falls, the contracts will be exchanged. The buyer purchases the property at the price they bid - this cannot be negotiated and the stipulated terms cannot be changed. The buyer will then pay 10% of the purchase price on the day and completion occur 28 days later. The funds are then paid to the seller less the fees of the Auctioneers and those of the seller's solicitor.

The atmosphere of an auction room can be extremely exciting and competitive and it is often the case that an interested party will bid in excess of the figure that had previously been set as their maximum. In some cases, the prices achieved at auction can be higher than those achieved by private treaty.

Now read the main points from chapter 1 overleaf.

****

Main points from chapter 1

❖ An auction sale facilitates the quick sale of a property, with sale and completion often taking place within one month of the successful bid.

❖ All sorts of property is suitable for auction and there are a variety of reasons for selling properties..

❖ Auction houses vary in size and the amount of business that they conduct and the frequency with which they hold auctions. Most will sell both residential and commercial property and each will have its own style of operation, and fee structure.

❖ All sorts of people attend auction, from investors to institutions to potential owner occupiers. The common denominator is that they are all interested in buying property.

Chapter 2

Selling at Auction

Advantages of selling at an auction

An auction is an efficient and cost effective way of selling property and if prepared properly with intensive marketing, advertising and mailing, will result in the greatest possible exposure of the lots offered. To maximize the effectiveness of the marketing, considerable thought must be given to the guide price, which needs to be tailored to generate competitive bidding in the auction room, thus ensuring that the best price is being achieved. Although some properties are more suitable for sale by private treaty, taking this route does present uncertainties over terms such as sale price and timing of exchange and completion.

Selling by auction however, offers a high degree of certainty that a sale will be achieved on a given day and, significantly, on the fall of the gavel an immediate binding contract is formed. As no further negotiation is permitted the entire sale process, from instruction to exchange of contracts can be achieved within as little as four weeks.

For vendors with a large number of properties to sell, auctions provide a highly efficient method of sale allowing for a total or phased disposal programme selling in individual lots thus maximising receipts. For those selling in a fiduciary capacity, there is the added advantage of the sale being entirely open and transparent. Most types of property are suitable for auction provided that a realistic reserve price is agreed.

Who sells at auction?

Auction is now regarded as the optimum method of sale for many sellers who range from private investors and property companies to banks, housing associations and local authorities.

When do you want to sell?

Decide when you want to sell your property and which auction you would like to put it in. Sale dates and venues can be found on auctioneer's websites. See appendix 1 for a list of auction houses.

What information do auctioneers need?

In order to give you the best possible advice auctioneers will need the following details:

Address
Description
Photograph
Tenure and Tenancy (if applicable) details
Floor plan or site plan
Anything else you consider to be material

Once the auctioneers have received this information, they will provide an estimate of the likely sale price of your property at Auction. Together with a proposed reserve, they shall send you a copy of their standard agency contract setting out their terms and conditions. Once the maximum reserve price is agreed you will be asked to sign and return the standard agency contract to confirm your instructions, at which time the Entry Fee becomes payable.

Proof of identity

If an auctioneer has not sold for you before they will require proof of your identity and address before they can market your property.

How much does it cost?

Auction Entry Fee

All auctioneers will charge a fee to enter a property into an auction. This fee is payable whether the property is sold or not. The fee is a contribution towards the cost of marketing and catalogue production. The fee will depend on how much space is taken in the catalogue for the property.

Commission

In the event of a sale, an auctioneer's commission is up to 2% of the sale price plus VAT for a sole agency or 2.5% plus VAT for a joint agency. A joint agency is usually advisable where the auctioneer feels it is necessary to include a local estate agent to handle local enquiries and conduct viewings. The auction house surveyors will confirm the auction entry fee and commission rate with you in writing before accepting your instructions.

Sales particulars

Once the auctioneer has been formally instructed, the property will be inspected by one of their surveyors, measurements taken where appropriate, and the property will be photographed. Draft sales particulars will then be forwarded to you and to your solicitors for approval and/or amendments.

Legal documents

At the same time your solicitors will be instructed to prepare a legal pack containing special conditions of sale, title documents, leases (where applicable), searches, planning documentation and office copy entries so that they are available to interested parties either by post or on line.

Guide price

The auction team will recommend a guide price which you will need to approve before marketing begins. It is important to set the guide price at a realistic level which is attractive to buyers. This will generate competitive bidding in the auction room and ensure that best value is achieved.

Marketing your property

Marketing will usually start approximately three to four weeks prior to the auction sale. Auction Houses produce thousands of catalogues for each auction. These are sent to prospective buyers such as private investors, property companies and developers.

E-marketing

Catalogues are available online and auctioneers send regular email alerts to the private investors who are registered on the site.

Advertising and PR

Good auctioneers will advertise in the key property publications and place advertisements in local newspapers.

Targeted Marketing

Auction houses also target individuals who have previously expressed an interest in similar properties, as well as adjacent occupiers, local agents, local developers, builders and property companies.

Viewings and Surveys

Potential purchasers may want to view your property during the marketing period and have a survey carried out. You should let the auctioneer know how you would prefer viewings to be arranged and we shall arrange access for buyers. In most cases, vacant properties are open at pre-arranged times for viewing. Details will be printed in the catalogue.

Legal documentation

In conjunction with your solicitors the auction house will supply copy documents to prospective purchaser's solicitors and will keep you constantly updated as to the levels of interest shown.

The reserve price

The auction House will agree a reserve price with you for your property a few days before the auction. This is the level below which they will not be authorised to sell. It is important that this be set at a realistic level.

Auction day

The Fall of the Gavel

On the fall of the Auctioneer's gavel, a binding contract is effected. The successful bidder is required to provide the name, address and telephone number of the purchaser and the purchaser's solicitors. The successful bidder will also be asked to provide a deposit for 10% of the purchase price. Identification of the purchaser is always checked at this stage. Clearance of all deposit cheques is arranged immediately after the auction.

Exchange of Contracts

The Memorandum of Sale is made up in the room and given to the purchaser to sign. The exchange is overseen by the auction house's solicitor. They will forward the purchaser's signed Memorandum of Sale to your solicitor. Completion will usually, take place 20 working days later. The deposit funds are then paid to you less fees.

What happens if the property does not sell on the day?
If your property fails to reach its reserve in the room, someone may still wish to buy it. You will need to decide whether to accept any offer and advise the auction house accordingly. The property may even be sold in the days or weeks after the sale as most auction houses continue to market the property.

Now read the Main Points from Chapter 2 overleaf.

****

Main points from chapter 2

❖ An auction is an efficient and cost effective way of selling property and if prepared properly with intensive marketing, advertising and mailing, will result in the greatest possible exposure of the lots offered.

❖ To maximize the effectiveness of the marketing, considerable thought must be given to the guide price, which needs to be tailored to generate competitive bidding in the auction room, thus ensuring that the best price is being achieved.

❖ All auctioneers will charge a fee to enter a property into an auction. This fee is payable whether the property is sold or not.

❖ On the fall of the Auctioneer's gavel, a binding contract is effected. The successful bidder is required to provide the name, address and telephone number of the purchaser and the purchaser's solicitors. The successful bidder will also be asked to provide a deposit for 10% of the purchase price. Identification of the purchaser is always checked at this stage. Clearance of all deposit cheques is arranged immediately after the auction.

...ction

We have seen how properties are sold at auction. It is significantly easier to sell than to buy property at auction, because of all the background work that is needed before deciding to bid. Of course this depends on what you want to do with a property once you have bought it. The following chapters deal with the process of bidding for a property and everything that underpins this. This chapter deals with the general process at auction.

How and why do I buy at auction?

Buying at auction is an assured way of securing a purchase. Once a bid is accepted, contracts will be exchanged on the day of the sale. The seller cannot withdraw from the sale, nor is it possible for any kind of gazumping to take place. Due to auctions being conducted in public, there can be no secret bidding or unfair competition and once the gavel comes down, the successful bidder is legally committed to pay the agreed price and complete the purchase. Another attraction of buying at auction is that properties are usually offered at a realistic guide price, particularly when in need of repair, refurbishment or being sold by a financial organisation to recover debts.

Why is property being sold at an auction?
There are a number of reasons why property is sold at an auction:

- A quick sale is needed, often due to the owner being in financial difficulties or it is a repossession

- There are structural problems which prevent the property being sold easily in the conventional manner.

- Properties sold by public bodies. here you get all sort of property, including weird and wonderful properties such as public toilets and police stations, all of which may have their uses.

- The property is unique and there are no direct comparisons, such as lighthouses and the above mentioned public toilet.

It is always best to find out why exactly the property is being sold at auction. Is it so difficult to get rid of because of some inherent reason. Ask why is this property at auction and not being sold in the conventional way? Who exactly is the vendor and what if any are the problems stopping it being sold conventionally?

The reasons that the property is at auction may be entirely innocent but it is always worth finding out to avoid future problems.

The seller will provide a legal pack that may be inspected at any time. Auctioneers will strongly advise that professional advice is obtained from a legal representative. Details of the seller's solicitors will be available and, should a mortgage be required, it is available to have this in place prior to the sale. Again, Auctioneers strongly advise that funding is discussed with a professional advisor prior to attending the sale.

The successful buyer will be required to pay 10% of the purchase price on the day, together with a buyer's premium which is normally £250 including VAT. The balance of the purchase price is required on the agreed completion day and this is normally 28 days after the auction, however this can vary so best to check with the auction house.

What happens next?

Once you have found your auction, to receive a complimentary auction catalogue you should contact the Auctioneers and this will give the information about the properties being offered for sale. You can also download a catalogue from the auctioneers website. The catalogue includes descriptions of the available properties, legal information, viewing arrangements and a guide price, which is purely an indication of a realistic selling price. This should not be taken as a firm asking or selling price and should be relied upon as a guide only. Professional advice must be taken in relation to any lot in which there is an interest.

For lots where viewings are arranged, these are carried out on a block basis and are published in all advertising and in the auction catalogue. Any prospective purchaser is welcome at these viewings and should the scheduled appointments be inconvenient, alternative arrangements can be made. Any interest must be registered with the Auctioneers in order that prospective purchasers may be kept informed as to the progress of the sale.

How do prospective purchasers find out legal and survey information for the properties in which they are interested?

A legal pack is requested from each of the vendor's solicitors and this contains copies of all legal papers, which will be required by any prospective purchasers for them to make an informed decision regarding the purchase of any lot. The pack will include office copy entries and plans, the relevant local authority search, leases (if applicable), Special Conditions of Sale, replies to pre-contract enquiries and any other relevant documents. A copy of these legal packs can usually be obtained from auctioneers for a small charge. Should any additional information be required, the seller's solicitors are listed in the catalogue and can be contacted directly. All legal packs are available for inspection at each auction - any purchase at auction takes place under the assumption that all documentation and the terms of the contract have been read.

It is strongly recommended that any potential purchasers carry out full investigations for any lot in which they have an interest and a survey is an integral part of that investigation.

How is finance arranged?

Should a mortgage be required, approval in principle must be obtained prior to auction. Lenders are now familiar with the auction process and are usually willing to provide a mortgage offer for buyers intending to purchase at auction. A valuation and survey will be required along with legal evidence that there are no issues that will affect the value.

It is essential that the lender can provide funds within the timescale for completion. On the day of the auction, the purchaser will need to pay 10% of the purchase price and must ensure there are cleared funds to pay this amount. Sometimes, finance can be arranged through an Auctioneers on request.

Can lots be bought before auction?

Vendors may consider offers submitted before auction day. Any such offers need to be submitted in writing to an Auctioneers - this will be referred to the vendor and their instruction will be passed on to the prospective purchaser. Any offers will have to be unconditional and the buyer must be in a position to exchange contracts and pay the required deposit before auction day. With most auctioneers, no offers are considered within five days of the auction.

What happens on auction day?

Buyers should check on the day before the auction that any required lots are still available. Early arrival at the auction is recommended to ensure the Auctioneer's announcements are noted regarding withdrawn lots and changes in the order of the sale.

The Auctioneer will make pre-auction announcements regarding the conduct at auction. Knowledge of these is strongly recommended. The Auctioneer will start the bidding by invitation and bids can be made by raising either a hand or the catalogue. In most cases an auction number will be issued prior to the bidding which will identify your bid.

All bidders in the room will have an equal opportunity to bid and the auction team will be available for support. Once the desired price is reached, the Auctioneer will announce that the gavel is about to fall and the property will be deemed sold. The successful buyer will be the person with the highest bid at the time the gavel falls. Contracts are then exchanged and the successful purchaser will be invited to the legal desk to pay the 10% deposit, the buyers fee and to sign the sales memorandum.

What should I take with me to the auction room?

The items required are as follows:

- Deposit cheque or banker's draft for any potential purchase
- Identification - this is legally required under the money laundering regulations. Therefore a driving licence or passport is required and a current utility bill to show proof of residence.
- Details of solicitors acting on behalf of any potential purchaser.

What happens if a prospective purchaser is unable to attend the auction?

If prospective purchasers are unable to attend the sale, it is possible to bid in other ways:

- By telephone - the interested party will be telephoned as the lot is being auctioned.

By proxy in writing - a member of the auction team will represent the buyer, who has previously specified their maximum bid

In each case a registration form and cheque to cover the deposit and buyer's fee, are required prior to the date of the auction. A bidder's registration form is printed in the catalogue or alternatively can be obtained from the office

Will the property be insured when I purchase?

No - the purchaser at auction is responsible for obtaining Building insurance cover from the moment the property is deemed sold to them at auction.

Now read the main points from chapter 3 overleaf.

****

Main points from chapter 3

❖ Buying at auction is an assured way of securing a purchase. Once a bid is accepted, contracts will be exchanged on the day of the sale. The seller cannot withdraw from the sale, nor is it possible for any kind of gazumping to take place.

❖ Due to auctions being conducted in public, there can be no secret bidding or unfair competition and once the gavel comes down, the successful bidder is legally committed to both pay the agreed price and complete the purchase.

❖ It is always best to find out why exactly the property is being sold at auction. Is it so difficult to get rid of because of some inherent reason. Ask why is this property at auction and not being sold in the conventional way? Who exactly is the vendor and what if any are the problems stopping it being sold conventionally?

❖ Once you have found your auction, to receive a complimentary auction catalogue you should contact the Auctioneers and this will give the information about the properties being offered for sale. You can also download a catalogue from the auctioneers website.

❖ Buyers should check the day before the auction that any required lots are still available. Early arrival at the auction is recommended to ensure the Auctioneer's announcement are noted regarding withdrawn lots and changes in the order of the sale.

Chapter 4

How to Go About Finding a Property at Auction

There are many property auctions being held all over the UK every day. Where you choose to buy at auction very much depends on what you want to buy, what is the intended use for the property, residential investment, commercial investment or a property for your own home.

Most people tend to concentrate on the area that they know. However, a few adventurous souls will branch out further afield. In order to find out the whereabouts of property auctions you will want to get hold of one of the main publications such as *Property Auction News* which is a magazine devoted entirely to property auctions in the UK. You will have to pay for this magazine by subscription, details of which can be found at www.propertyauctionnews.co.uk. The organ of the surveying world, The Estates Gazette, which is a weekly publication also features some property auctions.

One other invaluable source of information is the Essential Information Group. This is the news source for serious investors at auction. It is subscription based.

The Essential Information Group was formed in 1990 to provide the property industry with detailed information as to the results of all London property auctions. It now covers the whole of the UK and is recognised as the industry standard for auction information and currently includes details on over 500,000 properties and over 35,000 lots each year worth in excess of £5.5 billion. A range of services are available and they work closely with over 450 different auction houses arranging the transmission of guide prices, results and the provision of catalogues for interested parties. They also host a variety of Premium Rate services including a LiveLink service where people can listen live to an auction via telephone, thus allowing as many people as possible to access these auction details. The EIG have close ties with many auction houses where they provide services for viewing live property auctions on the internet. You can check out their online auctions page to see what auctions are going to be broadcast live. For more information on the Essential Information Group you should contact the address and website below.

By Post	By Phone	By Email
Essential Information Group Charter House 9 Castlefield Road Reigate Surrey RH2 0SA	01737 226150 Fax: 01737 242 693	Account Enquiries: accounts@eigroup.co.uk Sales and subscription enquiries: sales@eigroup.co.uk

Once you have found the auction houses(s) that you want to deal with you can go on their mailing list. There is a list of auction houses in the appendix with contact details. There are a number of websites which provide free auction lists, such as www.propertyauctionaction.co.uk. You can also often find auction catalogues online at the auction house website.

Repossessions

The slow housing market and an increase in repossessions have led to more buyers turning to auction houses. But while you may be able to pick up a discount, there are risks involved.

For people interested in buying, seeking out a repossessed home represents a real opportunity to snap up a property at a discount. However, you need to know where to look - and also consider the risks involved, especially if you are planning to buy through an auction.

Where to find repossessed property

The repossession process is fairly complicated, and begins when a homeowner gets into difficulties meeting their monthly repayments

After a lender has taken possession of a property, it is likely to appoint an asset manager to ensure it is empty, clean and ready to sell. The property will then either be put on the market through an estate agent or sold directly through an auction. The method of selling the property will depend on its value in the market; if the lender is looking for a quick sale, it may opt for an auction. However, if it feels the property is likely to attract a lot of attention, it may decide an estate agent is the best way to achieve a sale.

You can use a new website, propertyearth.net, which lists around a thousand chain-free properties, including repossessed flats and houses, probate homes and unsold new homes from property developers.

The website allows you to search for property by price, postcode or description; when you find one you like, you simply contact the estate agent involved. The one thing every home has in common is that there is no chain involved.

Auctions, meanwhile, might be more useful because the process can be a lot quicker – once the hammer falls the lot is technically yours and the sale then has to complete within 28 days.

Another advantage of buying at auction is that you can usually get a good deal – while there are no exact figures on this, experts generally say buyers can save up to 30%. However, the actual price you achieve will depend on the type of property, why it is being sold at auction and how many people are interested – a lot of competition could drive up the price.

Perusing the auctioneers catalogue
An auction house will release their catalogue several weeks before the auction begins . The catalogue will be in hard copy form or electronic form. This doesn't give much time for the prospective purchaser to look at what is on offer and arrange a viewing. and get everything else in order. However, that is the nature of auctions. Quick processes and quick disposals.

Below is an extract from an auctioneers catalogue (www.eddisons.com). This is an online catalogue so there will be references to 'click here' for further information.

See overleaf

Lot No:203 Guide Price (£): 115,000 - 120,000*

Viewing Details

Date	Time
2nd Sep 2014	14:00
9th Sep 2014	14:00
17th Sep 2014	14:00

The former Halton Wine and Food Store, 21-23 Chapel street, Halton, Leeds, LS15 7RN.

Status: Available

Category: Vacant Commercial

Venue (Auction)

Auction date: 18th September 2014

Instructed by: The Joint LPA Receivers

Details: vacant corner retail premises with spacious 4 bedroom residential accommodation over two floors-workshop and yard providing off street parking.

Location. the property occupies a prominent position on Chapel street in close proximity to the main shopping parade in Halton Leeds.

Ground Floor: retail Sales Area-extending to 49.79m2 (536ft2)

Residential accommodation-Lounge dining area kitchen WC

First floor-Four bedrooms (one with shower) bathroom WC

Outside-Secure gated yard providing parking for cars. Brick built garage/workshop

Note: All measurements are approximate and taken by a third party.

The above extract is typical of an auctioneers catalogue and provides enough detail for a prospective bidder to make up their mind to view. It is always very advisable indeed to view the property in question. Some don't and live to regret what they have bought. By viewing you can get an idea of what you are entering into and what you might need to spend bringing the property back into a condition where you can rent or sell (or live in).

The catalogue starts with the lot number and then a photo, usually one photo but sometimes more. the viewing dates are listed along with the address and the status, i.e. available, along with the category, in this case vacant commercial. The venue of the auction is mentioned and the date, along with who instructed the property to auction.

Then the catalogue will provide property details and location followed by more detail as to the property size and numbers of rooms, parking etc.

The information in the catalogue should provide sufficient detail to enable the prospective purchaser to go to the next stage and view the property then attend the auction.

The order of lots in the catalogue
An auction catalogue consists of Lots, and they will be numbered in the order at which they will be sold at auction. It is the practice of some auction houses to put the most popular lot at the start of the auction so as to draw bidders in. They will also intersperse less popular lots with the popular lots to ensure that bidder levels are maintained and people don't drift away after the 'sexy' lots have sold. It is important to remember that auction houses want to create an atmosphere of excitement on the day so that people will bid for what is on offer. Although people can bid by phone for a lot, still the most popular method

The guide price
The guide prices for properties at auction will vary, depending on what is for sale and where it is. Market forces will dictate this, as they do for property sold in the conventional way. However, for a good many properties the price will be set low, which reflects the condition of the property and also reflects the fact that the auctioneer wants to draw people in to bidding. In many cases, auctioneers will drop the guide price at the outset as most

people won't start bidding at the actual starting price. Therefore you will find that if a house is valued at £60,000 the auctioneer will open with this then drop down to £50,000 to start the bidding.

Guide prices are dictated by the reserve price on the lot. Sellers will have a price that they will not go under. This price is not disclosed to potential bidders before the auction but will affect the price at which the auctioneer starts the process. So, if a property is £60,000 and the auctioneer starts at £50,000 then £50,000 will be at the reserve price or just above.

Finding a property suitable for you in an auction catalogue
Once you have either been sent, or downloaded, a catalogue then you will need to identify the property or properties that you want to view and are interested in bidding for. There is quite a lot of background work to do before the auction begins. You will usually have about two weeks to start the ball rolling. After having identified a property suitable for you, you will need to arrange a viewing.

Viewing an auction property
As we have seen above with the auctioneers particulars, viewing times are usually set by the auction and shown in their catalogue and you will have to fit in with these times. They are very much like estate agents block bookings. The number of viewings are limited and you will usually get the opportunity to view three or four times before auction. The people who show the property will not usually have any idea about the details of the property, being employed as key holders to show interested parties around. They will take details of all those who have viewed. The viewings are in half-hour slots. Although the viewing times are stated in the catalogue it is always best to play safe and confirm the times as they can change. If you have travelled a long way to

attend a viewing only to find out it has been cancelled or rescheduled this can be very annoying, to say the least.

You will need to get used to the fact that if a property is popular and attracting lots of interest then there may be lots of people waiting at the property on the allotted day and time. However, you are there for a reason and need to keep your wits about you and take all the necessary notes. You will be greatly aided by doing adequate research , even before you get round to viewing the property.

When you go to a viewing make sure you have the following:

- A tape measure. Check the measurements against those stated in the auction catalogue. You can also use this date for your own plans.
- Camera. This probably goes without saying but you need to get accurate photos of the building, exterior and interior, to act as a record and help you with your own plans.
- A torch. The property may be dark inside and you need to know what you are looking at. Also, a torch may be needed for safety reasons, depending on the condition of the property.
- A note pad, or means of taking notes. This is very important as you may need to take copious notes to aid you in making your decision.
- If you can, take a small portable ladder. This should enable you to look into areas such as loft spaces or cupboards etc.

Using a surveyor
If you are not experienced in carrying out basic property surveys then you might want to employ the services of a surveyor. This might cost, but you will get a firm idea of the structural

condition of the property in question. You might want to do several viewings of the property, the first one yourself and then, if needs be, with a surveyor.

The notepad and camera will come in very useful the first time around. You should ensure that you take photos of the external and internal areas of the property. the following are areas that you will want to inspect, and which a surveyor would inspect:

- The envelope of the building. This includes the roof. You should check the roof timbers, tiles, condition of the covering such as the asphalt or felt and if it is a flat roof check for signs of standing water as this indicates that there are problems with the drainage. You might want to look at the eaves of the building, particularly if you wish to convert a loft or install a mansard (roof extension)
- Electrics and plumbing. With the plumbing you need to locate stopcocks and also ascertain the condition of the boiler. Check the external guttering and the condition of the soil stack. With the electrics check the age and state of the fuse board which will give you some idea of the state of the wiring. Check wall sockets and also check to see if you can see any wiring to ascertain the condition. Look into the loft to see if there are any wires running around. Whilst in the loft look at the existing loft insulation and also look up to see if you can see any daylight, which will indicate roof problems.
- Damp. Check for signs of damp-take photographs so you can ascertain whether it is rising or penetrating damp and just what the extent of work might be.
- Structure of the building. Look closely at the condition of the walls externally or whether there are any signs of movement or cracking and look for evidence of movement around door frames and windows and also floor levels.

- Gardens/outside spaces. These areas are quite often ignored by potential bidders. You should look at the condition of gardens, fences and also note any boundary lines. To refurbish an outside area takes a lot of time and money and you will want to get this right.

In addition to the above main points you should make a note of common areas if the property is a flat in a block. This will indicate the level of expenditure that might be need in the future and also how well kept the block is.

You should make a note of any parking arrangements and any pathways that run onto or close to your property. You might also want to have a look to see if the neighbours have carried out any alterations that you could also do to enhance the value of the property, such as an extension.

You may have read the above and decided that checking all of this and arriving at a plan or cost is a tall order. Which is why employing a surveyor might be very necessary. Employing a surveyor might cost about £250 plus VAT for a cursory inspection but it will be well worth it, particularly if you are not an experienced builder or are very experienced in the property game.

As we will see it might cost the same for an inspection of the legal documents but for if you are serious about a property and don't want to end up in trouble further down the line this is money well spent. There are a number of surveys available all with differing costs, as below.

Types of Surveys
The following gives a very brief overview of the different surveys available. When considering the possible purchase of the property the choices are as follows:

Full Building Survey   (most popular survey for most properties).

Homebuyer Report   (previously called a Homebuyer Survey and Valuation).

Valuation only.

Structural Inspection (General and Specific).

Home Condition Survey and RICS Condition Survey

Full Building Survey

A full Building Survey on an average house will cost in the order of £300 to £600. It will be carried out by a Chartered Surveyor who is a member of the Royal Institution of Chartered Surveyors (RICS). The Surveyor will normally look at the complete property and give a detailed opinion regarding the state of the building. This is probably now the most popular type of report. It is particularly suitable for older properties or properties which have had major alterations over the years or properties which appear to have problems that need further investigation.

Homebuyer Report or RICS Condition Report (previously called a 'Homebuyer Survey and Valuation')

A Homebuyer Report on an average house will cost in the order of £200 to £400. It will be carried out by a Chartered Surveyor who is a member of the Royal Institution of Chartered Surveyors (RICS) and is licensed to do this work. The Surveyor will normally look at the complete property and give an opinion as to whether or not the house is value for money to the purchaser. A Homebuyer Report is usually suitable if the house is of modern straight forward construction and has not had any major alterations carried out.

The old 'Homebuyer Survey and Valuation' report used to be very popular until the RICS informed their members that they could no longer carry it out. This has lead to a lot of confusion. It should be noted that a lot of Surveyors will carry out a report in the style of the old 'Homebuyer Survey and Valuation' report usually without the valuation. Talking to your chosen Surveyor about the different options is very much recommended.

Valuations

A Valuation only survey on an average house will cost the order of £150 to £300. It will usually be carried out by a Chartered General Practice Surveyor. This type of survey is usually done for the benefit of the mortgage lender.

General Structural Inspection

A General Structural Inspection on an average house will cost the order of £300 to £600. This will normally be performed by a Chartered Engineer who is a member of the Institution of Structural Engineers (IStructE) or the Institution of Civil Engineers (MICE). Some Chartered Surveyors also carry out these inspections. The inspection will concentrate only on the structural aspects of the building (foundations, walls and roof). It is often useful if the prospective purchaser is intending to carry out a total refurbishment and hence will be replacing the interior decoration and all the services (plumbing, electrics etc).

Specific Structural Inspection

A Specific Structural Inspection is sometimes called for when you have already had some sort of survey and the surveyor has identified a potential structural problem and recommends further investigation. It should be noted that if a Structural

Engineer is requested to look at a specific crack in a building then he will not necessarily look at any other part of the building.

Home Condition Survey and RICS Condition Report

A Home Condition Survey has some similarity to a Homebuyer Report but it does not address the question of value. These are carried out by Home Inspectors with the Dip HI qualification who are members of an accreditation scheme operated either by SAVA or the BRE. The RICS (Royal Institution of Chartered Surveyors) have also introduced an equivalent survey called a RICS Condition Report which is carried out by licenced Chartered Surveyor.

Other Reports

In some cases the Surveyor will recommend that further investigations should be considered. In some cases these would be highly recommended while in other cases they may be just noted and hence bought to your attention. Some of these possible extra investigations could include:

Electrical Report to check the state of the wiring, which if very old could be dangerous.

Drainage Report to check the drains, which if partly blocked may be causing subsidence.

Asbestos Report to check for asbestos content and make recommendations.

Arboricultural Report to make recommendations regarding any trees on the site.

General Tips

It can be useful if the homebuyer can be present while the Surveyor is performing the survey. Some Surveyors are positive towards meeting the homebuyer at the property but some Surveyors are not (understandably the presence of the homebuyer can often be a distraction). A useful compromise that many Surveyors recommend is for the homebuyer to meet the Surveyor at the property towards the end of his inspection. The Surveyor can then point out any particular observations on the spot, in advance of the production of the report. The homebuyer may also have questions along the lines of what are the possible costs for any remedial work that may be required etc.

If you are not able to meet the Surveyor at the site then of course the next best alternative would be to speak to the Surveyor on the telephone as soon as possible after the Survey. It should be remembered that Surveyors can survey a large number of houses in a week and it is not realistic to expect the Surveyor to give an off the cuff verbal report weeks later.

Before placing an order with a Surveyor you should always ask them to confirm that they have adequate qualifications, accreditation, experience and insurance to perform the work.

Obviously, underpinning your research is what exactly you want the property for, what is its purpose? Are you buying a property to live in, or to eventually sell for a profit or rent? You will need to do the sums to make sure that what you see is worth investing in and can be a viable rental proposition or there will be a profit when you sell. There are other areas of research for you to do when deciding this.

Using Google maps
I mention Google maps because it is now the most effective tool you can use to carry out fundamental research into a property and its location. Of course, you might have an intimate knowledge of an area and will not need to use this tool. If you

don't have this knowledge, you will want to find out where the property is in relation to transport links, industrial areas, schools, shops and other amenities which makes the property an attractive proposition and adds value. If you don't live in an area then Google maps Streetview function will enable you to walk along a street and see the area in more detail. Are there any houses which look derelict or might put prospective tenants or purchaser off, or would you want to live there yourself. If you are looking at a commercial property what kind of an area is it in, what catchment area does it serve?

The legal side of things
When a person buys a property through the conventional route, i.e. through an estate agent, each party to the transaction will have solicitors representing them. A good deal of time will be spent establishing the provenance of the property and establishing whether or not it is a sound purchase.

In an auction, as we have seen, when you bid for a property you will only have a maximum of 28 days to complete. Everything must be in place within this time frame. It is vital that you do all of your groundwork before the auction.

Most auction houses will allow prospective purchasers to download legal documents from their sites. This is known as the legal pack. You can do initial checks yourself, and if you feel that you need a solicitor to carry out further checks you can do so. the checks that you can do yourself consist of the following:

- Check to see that there is an Energy performance Certificate (EPC) with the pack. The EPC will tell you an awful lot about the property, the size, whether it is double glazed, the type of insulation, heating and so on. It will also indicate whether further measure need to be taken to improve the overall energy performance. You can factor any costs arising from this into your overall refurbishment budget.

- Title to property. This is most important. Right at the outset you will need to know the tenure of the property in question. Is it leasehold or freehold? Most people assume that houses are freehold and flats are leasehold. this is not always the case and there are areas in the UK with a large proportion of freehold flats, for example. This can have an effect on any resale plans as freehold flats can be notoriously difficult to manage and sell on. The data detailing the tenure of the property will come from the Land Registry. If the property is leasehold, the title documents will detail how long the lease is and what ground rent is payable. The legal information relating to a property is critical as it will indicate whether or not you should continue with the purchase, or the bidding, and what the costs may be when it comes to extending a lease. You can also see if there are any charges registered against a property, i.e. a mortgage lender. If you are unsure of anything it is always best to let a solicitor look at it and advise you. the cost is always worth it.

- Check to see how long the seller has actually owned the property. There are cases of people buying property and looking for a fast turnaround, *for one reason or another.* The reasons may be that they have bought something that is problematic and want it off their hands.

- Title plan. This is a simple drawing which will indicate boundaries of the property that you arc buying. Again, it is best, if you are unsure, to let a solicitor look at this. They usually have an expert eye and can spot things that you won't, such as access and right of way issues, flying freeholds (no mans land) etc.

- Service charges. My own background as a property manager has taught me that service charges can be one of the most contentious issues surrounding a property. Stories are legion of landlords charging exorbitant service charges and administration fees. There is also the problems of outstanding debts relating to a property that you have just purchased, or are about to bid for. There will be copies of service charge accounts and previous invoices paid on the property in the last three years (or there should be) plus there should be an estimate of future service charge expenditure. It is vital to see and understand this so you know what you are walking into and what you should budget for in the future. For example, this will have a bearing on what rent you can charge in the future and how payment of service charges can affect your profit margins.

Now read the Main points from Chapter 4 Overleaf

****

Main points from chapter 4

❖ There are many property auctions being held all over the UK every day. Where you choose to buy at auction very much depends on what you want to buy, what is the intended use for the property, residential investment, commercial investment or a property for your own home.

❖ The slow housing market and an increase in repossessions have led to more buyers turning to auction houses. But while you may be able to pick up a discount, there are risks involved.

❖ An auction catalogue consists of Lots, and they will be numbered in the order at which they will be sold at auction. It is the practice of some auction houses to put the most popular lot at the start of the auction so as to draw bidders in.

❖ The guide prices for properties at auction will vary, depending on what is for sale and where it is. Market forces will dictate this, as they do for property sold in the conventional way. However, for a good many properties the price will be set low, which reflects the condition of the property and also reflects the fact that the auctioneer wants to draw people in to bidding.

❖ Viewing times are usually set by the auction and shown in their catalogue and you will have to fit in with these time. They are very much like estate agents block bookings. The number of viewings are limited and you will usually get the opportunity to view three or four times before auction.

❖ If you are not experienced in carrying out basic property surveys then you might want to employ the services of a surveyor. This might cost, but you will get a firm idea of the structural condition of the property in question. You might want to do several viewings of the property, the first one yourself and then, if needs be, with a surveyor.

❖ Most auction houses will allow prospective purchasers to download legal documents from their sites. This is known as the legal pack. You can do initial checks yourself, and if you feel that you need a solicitor to carry out further checks you can do so.

Chapter 5

Obtaining Finance for an Auction Property

Financing an auction property

Property auctions have the main advantage that generally prices are lower (sometimes up to 50% lower) than high street estate agents. Also, the auction process is quick and produces an instant sale. You know you have bought the property once the hammer falls. No making offers and waiting for a response, or being gazumped at the 11th hour.

As we have discussed, properties that you would not see in the high street estate agents find their way into auctions: distressed sales and "fire sales", repossessions, run-down and derelict properties, and often properties at auction are in need of some repairs or refurbishment. You are dealing in the trade or "wholesale" market here and you need to be prepared to roll your sleeves up and get your hands dirty! But, there's lots of opportunity to get a bargain and then add value.

Buying at auction can be a more risky process: you really do need to know what you are doing, to have done your homework (due diligence) and to have your finance arranged beforehand.

Paying cash

Paying cash on the day is the ultimate way of buying an auction property. This gives you greater flexibility and more freedom and is cheaper as you are not paying and fees or interest and are not encumbered by the rules of lending organisations. However, not that many individuals have large quantities of cash to play with and therefore resort to borrowing the costs of purchase.

Borrowing money to fund a purchase

Once you spot the property you are interested in, you need to act fast as there will be a limited amount of time in which to do your due diligence research and arrange your finance before the auction takes place.

Property Auction Finance is normally based on the market value of the property, not the purchase price, which means if you spot a real bargain it is possible to achieve 100% funding on the purchase. It's vital that you are aware that normally you must pay a 10% deposit on the day of the auction. You have then committed yourself to going through with the total purchase within the timescale set - usually 28 days.

Finance can be arranged for residential and commercial property auction purchases. The type of finance that you need will depend upon the condition of the property you intend to buy and its subsequent use.

You will need to discuss your purchase plans with an advisor to agree a finance plan of action to ensure that the right auction funding is put in place, in time and also the most appropriate long-term solution. This process involves the preparation of a surveyor's valuation report:

Buy-to-Let Mortgages may be one solution and can sometimes be arranged within the timescale, but this may not always be the best solution.

Development or Refurbishment Finance is one answer when you need some minor or major work to the property. You may need property development finance in this situation. 100% financing can be arranged for viable schemes.

Bridging Finance is usually the preferred solution for auction purchases because of the timescale involved. This type of finance is quite appropriate for auction purchases and is not necessarily expensive. There are some very competitive deals available if you know where to source them.

Commercial mortgages and finance can be arranged for limited companies and for private individuals with good credit histories. Even those with problem credit histories, county court judgments (CCJ's), arrears or IVA's can be accommodated.

Property auction purchases have become more popular as demand for property and property investment has increase over the last 10 years or so. The number of properties sold at auction since 1999 has risen by around 70% - around 20,000 residential homes are now sold through UK auctions each year.

This has undoubtedly had an effect on prices and in some cases properties at auction have been fetching almost retail prices you would expect to pay in the high street.

All the more reasons to use caution when buying at auction: calculate exactly what the property is worth to you and don't pay more.

What you should do:

Do your estimates: building work, refurbishment and fitting out, letting costs, financing costs, legal and professional fees, plans drawing, planning and change of use costs, valuation costs. Know exactly what the project is likely to cost you then add 10% for contingencies.

Calculate your expected returns on the investment project and know exactly what the property is worth to you as an investment - don't get carried away and pay more.

Now read the main points from Chapter 5 overleaf.

****

Main points from chapter 5

❖ Paying cash on the day is the ultimate way of buying an auction property. This gives you greater flexibility and more freedom and is cheaper as you are not paying and fees or interest and are not encumbered by the rules of lending organisations. However, not that many individuals have large quantities of cash to play with and therefore resort to borrowing the costs of purchase.

❖ Once you spot the properties you are interested in, you need to act fast as there will be a limited amount of time in which to do your due diligence research and arrange your finance before the auction takes place.

❖ Property Auction Finance is normally based on the market value of the property, not the purchase price, which means if you spot a real bargain it is possible to achieve 100% funding on the purchase. It's vital that you are aware that normally you must pay a 10% deposit on the day of the auction. You have then committed yourself to going through with the total purchase within the timescale set - usually 28 days.

❖ Finance can be arranged for residential and commercial property auction purchases. The type of finance that you need will depend upon the condition of the property you intend to buy and its subsequent use.

Chapter 6

Doing Your Sums-What to Bid for a Property

What you intend to bid for a property will be the end result of what you have planned to do with it. If you are looking for an investment with a potential return then it is vitally important that you have a handle on all the costs involved, the costs of purchase (often overlooked) and the bid price plus any other costs of renovation.

The first thing to note is that not all properties will be financially viable. The actual cost of the property and the ultimate refurbishment costs might eliminate any profit. Unless of course you are bidding for a property that you intend to renovate and live in and are not bothered about value in the short term.

The next thing to consider when you have spotted a property is the costs of buying. There are a number of hidden costs to pay on top of the actual purchase price and any costs of renovation. he costs are as follows:

Stamp duty-this tax is paid by all purchasers of property, subject to the price of the property. The table below applies for all freehold residential purchases and transfers, whether and the premium paid for a new lease or the assignment of an existing lease.

Residential land or property SDLT rates and thresholds

Purchase price/lease premium or transfer value	SDLT rate
Up to £125,000	Zero
Over £125,000 to £250,000	1%
Over £250,000 to £500,000	3%
Over £500,000 to £1 million	4%
Over £1 million to £2 million	5%
Over £2 million	7%

If the value is above the payment threshold, SDLT is charged at the appropriate rate on the whole of the amount paid. For example, a house bought for £130,000 is charged at 1%, so £1,300 must be paid in SDLT. A house bought for £350,000 is charged at 3%, so SDLT of £10,500 is payable.

Higher rate for corporate bodies
From 20 March 2014 SDLT is charged at 15% on interests in residential dwellings costing more than £500,000 purchased by certain non-natural persons. If you exchanged contracts on or after 21 March 2012 but before 20 March 2014 the earlier £2 million threshold for this charge will apply, subject to transitional rules.

"Non-natural persons" include companies, partnerships including a company and collective investment schemes. There are exclusions for trustees of a settlement, property rental businesses, property developers and traders, properties made available to the public, financial institutions acquiring dwellings in the course of lending, dwellings occupied by employees and farmhouses.

Annual Tax on Enveloped Dwellings is a tax payable by companies on high value residential property (a dwelling) and came into effect on 1 April 2013 and is payable each year.

Legal costs Sometimes with auction properties, one reason why they are being sold at auction is that there is a sticky legal problem to be resolved. There may be a need to extend the lease or sort out rights of way, whatever, it all adds up!

Costs of raising finance to purchase the property. As we know, there are costs to raising finance, such as administration costs, arrangement fees and a number of other ancillary costs that you need to be fully aware of.

Building survey-we have discussed the costs of the various types of survey-you need to decide whether you need a survey, what kind and factor this cost in.

Property insurance-when you buy property at an auction you will need to insure it from the day of exchange. If the property is empty then a higher premium for non-occupation will apply. You will need to ensure that all details, such as works to the property are communicated to the insurer. It is worth looking to see if the property, if leasehold, benefits from insurance under the freeholders policy.

How to determine what price to pay at the auction

As we have discussed, there are several motives for buying property at auction-personal dwelling or investment are two of the main motives. The starting point for any bid will be knowledge of the current value of the property as it stands at auction and the end value of the property once all the works are complete. The bit in the middle, the most important bit, is what are the costs of restoring the property to a good condition?

If the cost of the property plus the refurbishment costs are less than the value of the property in good condition then you have made, or can make, a profit. If you intend to rent out the property then you will want a healthy return on capital, which can be measured against the overall cost.

What you need to do is to understand the market local to the property that is being sold. You need to do your research and get to know comparable prices in the area. There are plenty of estate agents and the old method of foot slogging around them all will enable you to see the prices in an area. Alternatively you can do this from the comfort of your armchair by searching the web. The below represents a list of websites that can assist you in your research.

Rightmove-www.rightmove.co.uk. This is the biggest of them all and they have property for sale all over the UK. they have a number of useful tools such as a price comparison report, where you can see sold prices.

Zoopla-www.zoopla.co.uk likewise a leading site which is similar to Rightmove and also enables you to obtain comparisons.

Nethouseprices www.nethouseprices.com this site lists all the actual sold prices in the UK.

Property Price Advice www.propertypriceadvice.co.uk this site provides a basic online valuation of a property.

There are of course more sites which are roughly similar but the above will prove useful to your research.

There are also sites which can provide average property prices and market trends for different areas. These are useful if you are trying to track increases (or falls) in property prices. The House Price Index, which is based upon data from the Land Registry can be useful. See www.landregistry.gov.uk/public/house-prices-and-sales. The Registers of Scotland, which is the Scottish equivalent of the Land Registry provides a similar service. See www.ros.gov.uk.

The Halifax and Nationwide also have price indexes. See www/lloydsbankinggroup.com/media1/economic_insight/halifax_house_price_index_page.asp and www.nationwide.co.uk/hpi/defauklt.htm.

The more that you know about property prices and trends the better equipped you will be to understand exactly what you can bid for a property to make it viable.

In the final chapter of this book, I will be using a day at an auction to highlight all of the factors involved in the purchase of several residential properties and one commercial property. This includes calculations of all costs of purchase and renovation and likely profits.

Knowledge of the local area

Of course, if you are born and bred in the area where you intend to purchase property you will probably know and understand all the finer points of what to buy and where to buy, what can be rented out and so on. However, you may not know an area and need to undertake some research to gain knowledge. there are a number of sites which can assist you in this research.

UKLocalArea will enable you to get an idea of the profile of a neighbourhood. You type in a postcode and get back an immediate profile which includes schools, railway stations and other data such as local school performance. www.uklocalarea.com.

If you require more detailed statistics relating to an area, right down to birth and death rates go to www.neighbourhoodstatistics.gov.uk. For crime in an area see www.police.uk. For more details on specific schools you should visit the Ofsted website www.ofsted.gov.uk/inspection-reports/find-inspection-report.

There are other factors you may want to consider, such as the nature of the local environment which can be obtained from the Environment Agency www.environment-agency.gov.uk.

Calculating the cost of works to a property
Having looked at property research it is now time to get down to the nitty-gritty of calculating what works might be needed to bring a property up to standard. Only when you have done these sums can you know what it is worth bidding for a property. Again, in the final chapter there will be examples laid out.

If you have a builder friend or relative then this will save a lot of time and trouble. You can look at the property with them and arrive at a back of an envelope calculation. Builders usually know what they are talking about (most). However, if you are carrying out the initial survey yourself you will need to plan the works, i.e. know what you want and the property needs, for example if it is completely run down then new bathroom, kitchen, rewire, re-plastering, re-plumbing and so on, and then get a quote from an independent builder.

Lists of reputable builders can be obtained from your local authority or by visiting www.checkatrade.com. This site enables you to get in touch with builders who have passed their assessment and are recommended by them.

The best thing to do is to take a builder on site with you and give you an estimate then and there. Their estimate will not be exact and will not be binding but will enable you to see what kind of work is required. Other things to consider are what you want to get out of the building-do you want to sell for a profit and if so what standard of finish do you want? Do you want to rent it out and if so what standard of finish will you want? Do you want to live in it yourself, in which case you may want to arrive at a completely different standard of finish.

Selling costs

If you intend to sell a property after you have renovated it you will need to deduct the selling costs from your final profit. Selling costs can be quite hefty and can erode your profits quite heavily, particularly estate agents fees. It is often cheaper to use online agents although if you do you will need to arrange and undertake viewings yourself. When you watch programmes such as Homes Under the Hammer, the actual auction costs and other costs are never really highlighted. It is very important that you have a handle on all of the costs involved.

Calculating the bid price of a property

After you have undertaken all of your research, and know what the build and on-costs are, you should be in a position to know what you can bid for a property, what is your ceiling price. You will want to prepare a calculation that will aid you in this process, which is a simple list, as follows:

The market value of the property in its current state (£60,000) with discount applied this is £54,000.

The costs involved in buying (£3,800)

The costs of works to restore the property (£15,000)

Auction discount £6,000

Value of property when finished £95,000

(The auction discount is the reduction in price of the property when placed in the auction, typically 10%).

As you can see from this example, the initial bid price is £54,000. If you got the property for this (most bidding will start under this price) then your costs overall will be £78,800 to bring it up to market value of £95,000. Therefore there is a potential profit of £16,200 to be made. This will diminish as the bidding gets higher, if it gets higher so you will need to arrive at a point at which you will not go above. In this case, if £10,000 profit is your minimum then you wouldn't want to go above around £60,000.

By doing your sums this way, you will arrive at a fairly accurate figure which will inform your bidding. As far as costs go, it is always better to allow a bit more than you have anticipated as there will always be those problems that arise that you didn't foresee.

Rental yields and capital yields
The above represents the sale price of a property and the potential profit. However, you might be investing for a different reason, i.e. to rent out. You will also want to know what the capital appreciation is after all works.

Investment properties which are rented out receive an income from tenants. In order to calculate the gross rental yield the annual rental income is divided by the purchase price of the property (annual rent÷price) X 100 = Gross rental yield)

So, if the property was purchased for £75,000 (total) and the rent received is £450 per month the yield would be:

£5400 (annual rent) ÷ £75,000 X 100 which equals an annual yield of 7.2. This is a very respectable return on your capital. Of course if you are a landlord then you will want to factor in the costs of being a landlord, such as maintenance, insurance, loan costs, empty periods etc.

Capital yields
If and when a property increases with time, this is known as capital growth. A simple example is if you buy a property for £75,000 and it increases by 25% there will be a capital appreciation of £18,750. It is a rule of thumb that low price properties might produce a high rental yield and low capital growth and vice-versa, although this is not always the case. Again, each case differs and many factors will play a part but as long as you know what you want then you should be safe with your investment.

Buying property before auction
It is, of course, possible to purchase a property before it actually goes to auction. All of the conditions of sale in the auction room apply, the only difference being is that the property will be withdrawn from auction.

When buying before auction, you will need to find out from the auctioneer whether or not the buyer will accept a price before sale. If so you will then have to agree a price with the seller. the price will have to be attractive enough to persuade the seller to sell before auction. therefore, you will need to work out a price that is likely to be accepted. Again, using all the knowledge that you have gained from this chapter you should probably go towards your ceiling and make the offer. You will still, in most cases, be liable for auctioneers costs

Now read the main points from Chapter 6 overleaf.

****

Main points from chapter 6

❖ What you intend to bid for a property will be the end result of what you have planned to do with it. If you are looking for an investment with a potential return then it is vitally important that you have a handle on all the costs involved, the costs of purchase (often overlooked) and the bid price plus any other costs of renovation.

❖ The first thing to consider when you have spotted a property is the costs of buying. There are a number of hidden costs to pay on top of the actual purchase price and any costs of renovation.

❖ The starting point for any bid will be knowledge of the current value of the property as it stands at auction and the end value of the property once all the works are complete. The bit in the middle, the most important bit, is what are the costs of restoring the property to a good condition? If the cost of the property plus the refurbishment costs are less than the value of the property in good condition then you have made, or can make, a profit. If you intend to rent out the property then you will want a healthy return on capital, which can be measured against the overall cost.

❖ You also need to do your research and get to know comparable prices in the area

Chapter 7

The Day of the Auction

As you can see, an awful lot of time and effort goes into research and preparation when looking for suitable properties at auction.

The day of the auction
Having armed yourself with all you need to know about a particular property, it is assumed that you are comfortable with the property you have selected to purchase at auction and the auction day has arrived. Before you set off to the auction, phone the auction house to make sure the auction is still taking place at the published venue and time and that the lot you are interested in has not been withdrawn.

If you are successful in bidding for your lot then you will need to put down a deposit of ten percent. Sometimes if the value of the property is less than twenty thousand pounds then the minimum deposit is two thousand pounds. The deposit cannot be paid for in cash or credit card and you must take along two items for proof of identity such as a passport and utility bill.

Make sure you arrive at the auction at least an hour before the auction starts. This will give you time to register, if necessary, and to check any last minute special conditions relating to your lot. Some auction houses require you to register, then give you a card with a number on it so that if you are the successful bidder for a lot then you are easily identifiable. Familiarise yourself with the auction room and find a place where you have good vision of all the other bidders so you can get an idea of who is bidding against you.

The role of the auctioneer

In the auction room, the main person is the auctioneer. It is his or her skill in selling the property that dominates. It is the job of the auctioneer to get the highest price that they can for the property, both for the vendor and for their own fee income.

Auctioneers will have different styles of conducting sales depending on where the auction house is and the culture of a particular house. Their styles will range from the cajoling to try to get more bids, to the aggressive to try to at least rise above the reserve price.

Notwithstanding their own individual styles, they are all bound by a common code of conduct. The auctioneer will reserve the right to bid on behalf of the vendor. the auctioneer will state this in his or her opening words. What this really means in practice is that, if the bidding has not reached the reserve price then the auctioneer can take a bid 'off the wall' to try to up the bids to the reserve price. This is known as 'chandelier bidding'.

Bidding for your lot

You will want to be in a position where you can be clearly seen by the auctioneer. If you have a lot in your sights then you will want to ensure that, when the time comes for a bid you can be clearly seen and heard. The best tactic is to arrive as early as possible and to obtain a prominent seat, as close to the front as possible but not right at the front.

When the auction starts the auctioneer will direct you to a copy of the general conditions of sale for the auction but will not actually read them out. You should be familiar with them before the auction. The will briefly explain the bidding process and then the auction will begin. The auctioneer will give a very brief description of the lot and then ask for the bidding to begin. As a rough estimate the auctioneer will process between twenty and twenty-five lots per hour though this may vary.

When the auctioneer announces your lot it is time for you to go into action. Make sure you bid clearly so that the auctioneer registers your bid. The old myth that if you scratch your nose you have made a bid is not true. Your bid will only be registered if the auctioneer sees a definite gesture. The bidding process is quite organised with the auctioneer only ever registering the bids of two people until one drops out and then they look for another bidder. You may not even get to bid if the current bidders go above your ceiling. Telephone bids are quite common with someone from the auction house bidding on behalf of the person on the telephone. Quite often the auctioneer will open the bidding with one person making a bid and then no other bids until the auctioneer has announced the property will be sold on the third and final asking.

At this point just as the hammer is about to come down someone makes a bid and the bidding war starts. Keep in mind the ceiling price that you calculated before the auction and stop bidding when the price gets to your limit. Do not get carried away with the emotion of the auction room and start bidding above the limit you set yourself before the auction. If you are successful in your bid for your desired lot then you may be asked to hold up the card with the number given to you when you registered for the auction and a member of the auction house staff will come to find you.

Bidding in increments

What to bid is quite important. If you think that the property is yours if you bid way above the reserve price too soon then you might find that you have paid too much. Better bidding in increments to keep the rises in check. You can bid late by jumping in at the last moment, taking everyone by surprise and knocking them off balance. In this way you can achieve what you want. My own recent experience suggest that you can gain what you want by bidding late but then bidding in small increments.

There will be some forms to fill in and the deposit to be paid plus a fee to the auction house that is usually up to £750 although this will vary and can be lower or higher. You should ensure that you have the following on you when you go to auction:

- Photographic proof of identification. This can be a passport or driving licence
- Proof of residential address with a bill or bank statement dated within the last three months
- Cleared funds, i.e. proof that you can pay your 10% deposit then and there.

The balance of the money will be required to be paid by you within twenty-eight days although sometimes you may have to complete within fourteen days if stipulated by the vendor. Make sure your solicitor is aware that time is of the essence and that you need to complete quickly.

Unsold property at auction

Around three quarters of all property at auction is usually sold. This will depend on the auction and what is for sale. However, If the bids for a property are not accepted because they do not reach a level close enough to the reserve price that has been set for the property then the lot will be withdrawn from the auction (sometimes left to the auctioneers discretion at the instruction of the seller). If you are still interested in the property then see the auctioneer after the auction. There may be a deal to be done with the vendor. Many buyers will do a deal with the seller after the auction if the property remains unsold. This is known as 'Hawking'. If you buy after auction then auction conditions still apply and time is of the essence. If others are interested in the same property, it is the first person to submit money and exchange contracts who will win.

Withdrawn property

Sometimes and for no apparent reason the property that you are interested in might be withdrawn. This could be that the vendor has sold pre-auction or that there are problems with the estate. If you have spent any money prior to auction on checking the property out, either surveyors costs or legal costs, then you will lose this as the vendor has no responsibility for any losses incurred.

Now read the main points from chapter 7 overleaf.

****

Main points from chapter 7

❖ Before you set off to the auction phone the auction house to make sure the auction is still taking place at the published venue and time and that the lot you are interested in has not been withdrawn.

❖ If you are successful in bidding for your lot then you will need to put down a deposit of ten percent. Sometimes if the value of the property is less than twenty thousand pounds then the minimum deposit is two thousand pounds. The deposit cannot be paid for in cash or credit card and you must take along two items for proof of identity such as a passport and utility bill.

❖ In the auction room, the main person is the auctioneer. It is his or her skill in selling the property that dominates. It is the job of the auctioneer to get the highest price that they can for the property, both for the vendor and for their own fee income.

❖ When the auctioneer announces your lot it is time for you to go into action. Make sure you bid clearly so that the auctioneer registers your bid. The old myth that if you scratch your nose you have made a bid is not true. Your bid will only be registered if the auctioneer sees a definite gesture.

❖ What to bid is quite important. If you think that the property is yours if you bid way above the reserve price too soon then you might find that you have paid too much. Better bidding in increments to keep the rises in check.

Chapter 8

Procedure After the Auction

For those who have bought their first property at auction, the first feeling is usually one of elation and success. For the more seasoned, well it's just another day. Whatever, there will be the business to be taken care of.

Exchange of contracts
I have emphasised throughout the book that as soon as the gavel falls the buyer must be in the position to exchange contracts. The moment that a contract is formed is the moment that the auctioneer brings down his gavel. What happens after the auction is that a memorandum will be signed which is a brief contract and constitutes exchange of contracts. Importantly here, the auctioneer has the legal right to sign the contract on behalf of buyer and seller. This is convenient in that if either the buyer or seller cannot be present at the auction the auction house can take care of the business. Once the auction is complete a member of the auction house staff will find you and accompany you to sign contracts. See overleaf for a sample Memorandum of sale.

SAMPLE AUCTION SALES MEMORANDUM

THE LOT	
THE PRICE (EXCLUDING VAT)	£
DEPOSIT PAID	£
BALANCE PAYABLE	£
NAME AND ADDRESS OF SELLER	
NAME AND ADDRESS OF BUYER	
NAME AND ADDRESS OF BUYERS SOLICITORS	
THE SELLER AGREES TO SELL AND THE BUYER AGREES TO BUY THE LOT FOR THE PRICE. THIS AGREEMENT IS SUBJECT TO THE CONDITIONS SO FAR AS THEY APPLY TO THE LOT. WE ACKNOWLEDGE RECEIPT OF THE DEPOSIT	
SIGNED BY THE SELLER	
DATE	
SIGNED BY US AS AN AGENT FOR THE SELLER DATE	

This memorandum includes the auction lot number, address of lot, price payable and deposit paid. One copy is signed and dated by or on behalf of the buyer and one copy will be signed by or on behalf of the vendor. the two documents are then exchanged. Bingo! Exchange of contracts. There is no way out from this point. You are legally bound.

It is at the memorandum stage that you provide identification and pay deposit and also buyers premium. It is also the time for you to appoint solicitor, if one is not already waiting in the wings. You will also need to inform whichever finance company is funding the purchase. Insurance should also be arranged.

If you are delayed or can't complete
Because we don't live in a perfect world, sometimes delays might occur in the purchase of the property. This is usually for finance reasons. The sale contract will lay out penalty's which will have to be paid if the contractual completion date is overrun. If this is going to happen to you should always let your solicitor know so that he or she can sort it out.

If the sale cannot be completed, this is where things can get very complicated. You will lose your deposit for certain. If the vendor resells the property and the sale proceeds are less than what he would have got from selling to you then the vendor is entitled to take legal action against you to recover the difference between what he has sold it for and the price agreed by you.

There are very few occasions where you can get out of the purchase. It is the full responsibility of the buyer to carry out all checks necessary before bidding for a property. The Property Misdescriptions Act 1991 can apply if the property has been grossly misrepresented but Auction houses usually have everything sewn up in regard to this. If you do believe that a property has been misrepresented then you will have to inform your solicitor of this straight away before finally completing the sale.

Now read the main points from Chapter 8 overleaf.

****

Main points from chapter 8

❖ As the gavel falls the buyer must be in the position to exchange contracts. The moment that a contract is formed is the moment that the auctioneer brings down his gavel. What happens after the auction is that a memorandum will be signed which is a brief contract and constitutes exchange of contracts.

❖ It is at the memorandum stage that you provide identification and pay deposit and also buyers premium. It is also the time for you to appoint solicitor.

❖ If the sale cannot be completed, this is where things can get very complicated. You will lose your deposit for certain.

Chapter 9

A Day at The Auction.

We attended an auction held by Graham Penny at Nottingham Racecourse on the 17th of October 2014, commencing at 11.30am. There were approximately 40 lots on offer in the catalogue although 4 had been withdrawn on the day.

We registered for the auction and gave all details and showed proof of identity. We also had to provide proof that we had solicitors instructed before we could bid. In case we didn't have solicitors there were several firms offering their services. there were also other firms in attendance offering finance and building services.

The auction was well attended, with about 140 people occupying a room holding 100 seated. There were several telephone bidders to the left of the room. The auction was being filmed for 'Homes Under the Hammer' to be aired sometime in the future.

Bidding for lots
My business partner and I found two properties in the auction catalogue that we were interested in bidding for, a three bed semi detached property in a fairly poor state of repair with a

guide price of £68,000 and a two/three bed structurally detached property in (very) poor state of repair for £45,000.

Three bed semi-detached

This property would be ideal for rental purposes and, although it needed approximately £6,000 spent on it would seem to offer both capital growth and an average rental yield. We used various sites, mentioned in the previous chapter, to ascertain that the neighbourhood is sound and free from crime, there were good local amenities such as transport and schools and there were no adverse works planned which could affect the price of the property. Therefore, we decided that the property would be a good investment for sale or rent.

As I am a property manager, we dispensed with the services of a surveyor and carried out our own cursory survey on the viewing day. Although there were people swarming over the property we still managed to come up with a credible plan. We judged that the following needed to be done to the property to bring it back up to a high standard, in keeping with the rest of the properties in the street:

NEW KITCHEN
NEW BATHROOM AND SHOWER
NEW BOILER
SOME REPAIR WORK FROM INGRESS OF DAMP FROM THE ROOF
MINOR REPAIRS TO THE ROOF
FULL DECORATION THROUGHOUT
GARDEN TIDYING UP AT REAR
FULL REWIRE

TOTAL £6,000

Research on Rightmove showed that a similar property in the same street sold in June 2014 for £115,000. We believed we could achieve £120,000. In terms of capital growth and profit from instant sale, the following were our calculations:

Cost of property at auction £96,000 against £68,000 guide price.

Legal costs £950 plus VAT (£1240)

2.5% auction fee £750plus VAT = £900

TOTAL £98,140

Costs of refurbishment

£6,000

Total £104,140

Costs of sale

Priced at £125,00 to achieve £120,00

Estate agents fees 2% Say sale at £120,000 = £2400 plus VAT = £2880

Legal fees £1200 including VAT

No finance fees as we would pay with cash. However, it is important if you are using borrowed money to factor the costs of finance in.

Total £4080

Total sale profit

Costs of purchase and refurbishment £104,140

Sale price £120,000

Costs of sale £4080

Potential Profit £11,780

Therefore the property would achieve a healthy profit. Don't forget to factor in any other costs such as buildings insurance. Lets look at the rental yields available.

Rental yields

Research on Rightmove and Zoopla revealed that the rental returns on this type of property would be around £500-550 per calendar month.

The following costs would be associated with rental:

Buildings Insurance £200 per year

Initial costs of furnishing property (white goods) £750

Annual gas and electric checks £300

Costs of agency if using agency to find tenant (initial £500 plus VAT)

There would be a monthly management fee of around 10% to factor in if using an agent to manage the property.

In this case there are no mortgage costs as we would pay cash, however, in many cases there is a monthly mortgage payment to consider.

Rental yield

As we have seen the rental yield is calculated by annual rental (£6000) divided by the price (£104,140) times 100 = annual yield 5.76 per annum.

Given that we are using our own cash there are no hefty financing costs so the overall yield is very reasonable. However, taxation should be considered. It is very necessary to employ an accountant who is knowledgeable about the in's and out's of buy-to-let property accounting.

Overleaf-Lot 2.

Structurally detached two/three bed property

This property did not sell at the guide price of £45,000 and was eventually withdrawn. However, we have calculated a potential return below as if it had sold at £60,000. We carried out the same checks as before regarding neighbourhood and general area, which revealed that the property was in a very desirable area. However, the low price reflected the very run down state of the property. 'Structurally detached' means that, although the property abuts the adjacent house it is in fact detached from it. As before, we dispensed with the services of a surveyor and carried out our own cursory survey. We judged that the following needed to be done to the property to bring it back up to a high standard.

NEW KITCHEN
NEW BATHROOM AND SHOWER
NEW BOILER NEW RADIATORS
NEW ROOF (WELSH SLATE)-New rainwater goods
FULL DECORATION THROUGHOUT
GARDEN SIGNIFICANT WORK AT REAR (garden 150 feet by 50 feet) DEMOLITION OF OUTBUILDINGS

FULL REWIRE
NEW WINDOWS AND DOORS

In addition to the usual works we judge that this property, which was extremely spacious, could be remodelled to achieve a smaller bathroom and a sizeable third bedroom. This could be achieved by demolishing a chimney breast and reducing the size of the bathroom.

The photo below indicates the size (and condition) of the bathroom.

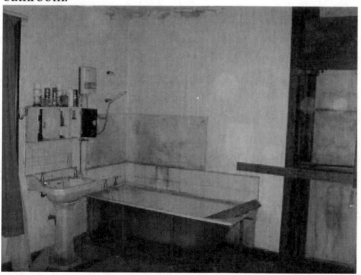

The above bathroom is 10 feet 10 inches by 12 feet 10 inches and could easily be converted into a bedroom by moving a wall to the side (bedroom) reducing both bathroom and bedroom to create a third bedroom. This could be achieved without drastically reducing the overall layout.

An extension could be built at the rear to enhance the ground floor, although this hasn't been factored into the costing. It would be necessary to obtain alternative valuations with the property extended to see if it is worth going down that route.

TOTAL £38,000 with a £5000 contingency for cost overruns.

Although this was an unusual property, and very spacious by normal standards, research on Rightmove showed that a fairly similar property in the same area sold in June 2014 for £120,000. Given the unusual nature and location of this property and the size of the garden, we were certain that we could obtain around £125,000.

In terms of capital growth and profit from instant sale, the following were our calculations:

Cost of property at auction £60,000 (final sale cost)
Legal costs £950 plus VAT (£1240)
2.5% auction fee £750plus VAT = £900

TOTAL £62,140

Costs of refurbishment

£43,000 (including contingency costs)

Total £105,000

Costs of sale

Priced at £130,000 to achieve £125,00

Estate agents fees 2% Say sale at £125,000 = £2500 plus VAT = £3000

Legal fees £1200 including VAT =£1440

No finance fees as we would pay with cash. However, it is important if you are using borrowed money to factor the costs of finance in.

Total £4,440

Total sale profit

Costs of purchase and refurbishment £103,000

Sale price £125,000

Costs of sale £4,440

Potential Profit

£20,560

Therefore the property would achieve a very healthy profit indeed. Don't forget to factor in any other costs such as buildings insurance.

Rental yields

Research on Rightmove and Zoopla revealed that the rental returns on this type of property would be around £700-750 per calendar month. As this is a one off property, unusual in its nature, very attractive with a huge garden, we thought that a higher than average rental for the area could be obtained.

The following costs would be associated with rental:

Buildings Insurance £300 per year

Initial costs of furnishing property (white goods) £750

Annual gas and electric checks £300

Costs of agency if using agency to find tenant (initial £750 plus VAT)

There would be a monthly management fee of around 10% to factor in if using an agent to manage the property.
In this case there are no mortgage costs as we would pay cash, however, in many cases there is a monthly mortgage payment to consider.

Rental yield

As we have seen the rental yield is calculated by annual rental (say £725 = £8700) divided by the price (£103,000) times 100 = annual yield 8.44 per annum.

Given that we are using our own cash there are no hefty financing costs so the overall yield is very reasonable. However, taxation should be considered. As we stated above, it is very necessary to employ an accountant who is knowledgeable about the in's and out's of buy-to-let property accounting.

The companion volume to this book, A Straightforward Guide to Letting Property for Profit goes into letting property and taxation issues in more depth.

As a footnote, although we bid for both of the properties we didn't buy either as the bidding exceeded our ceiling in the case of the first property and the second was withdrawn. However, our calculations made both an attractive investment for us.

****

Conclusion

As you might have gathered by reading this book, although actually buying a property at auction is really just a case of bidding for it, actually knowing what property to buy and what to bid, and what is your ceiling price is the end result of careful research.

You need to know everything about the property and the area that it is in. True, people bid blindly at auction but even they have some idea of what they are buying.

Essentially, you need to look for properties that are sold at an undervalue, you need to know what the refurbishment costs are and what the costs of purchase and sale are (if you intend to sell). If you intend to rent you need to know what the potential rental yield is after costs.

To make a successful bid at auction and then go on to make a profit, or gain a decent rental income and capital growth requires prior knowledge of what you are buying and what the area is like, indeed what the town or city is like and what kind of tenants or buyers can be attracted.

Like many things in life, experience counts for a lot in the property auction world. You need to understand the source of finance, building costs and something about building defects. Given that you are making a big investment you need to get it right.

I hope that this brief book has given you an insight into the world of property auctions and also an idea of what you need to do, and what background work is required when purchasing a property at auction.

Auction Glossary of terms

Actual completion date
The date when completion takes place or is treated as taking place for the purposes of apportionment and calculating interest.

Addendum
An amendment or addition to the conditions whether contained in a supplement to the catalogue. This may be a written notice in the catalogue, or announced at the auction.

Auction
A public sale in which property or items of merchandise are sold to the highest bidder.

Auctioneer
The person who conducts an auction. The auctioneer introduces each lot offered for sale, acknowledges bids, and announces whether lots are sold or unsold and their final bid prices.

Auction catalogue
The catalogue gives a description of the property, details on how to view each property and the General Conditions of Sale. These are prepared by the auctioneer, stating the basis on which the auction is carried out.

Bid
The offer to buy property at a specific price.

Completion
On completion of the sale of the lot there is usually a defined time period from the auction to the completion date in which the sale must be finalised. Penalties will be applied if the sale is completed late which can include losing your deposit.

Exchanging contracts

If you are the successful bidder at the auction sale, the sale is binding on the fall of the hammer and you will then be asked to sign and exchange contracts in the auction room.

Guide price

A guide price gives an indication of the price that the property is expected to sell for and what the vendor is hoping to achieve.

Guide prices are for information only and shouldn't be relied on as an indication of reserve price, or representing professional valuations for any purpose. Purchasers are deemed to have relied on their own knowledge or obtained the independent, professional advice of others.

In the room

A bid from someone in the room (not by phone.)

Legal pack

The vendor's solicitors prepares a legal pack containing copies of all the legal papers that you and your solicitor are likely to need to make an informed decision about your lot. The pack should include (where applicable) copies of: special conditions of sale, title deeds, leases, office copy entries, searches, replies to pre-contract enquiries. All legal packs will be available for inspection at the auction room. You must be aware that you buy subject to all documentation and terms of contract whether or not you have read them.

Lot

Each separate property described in the catalogue or (as the case may be) the property that the seller has agreed to sell and

Previews or exhibitions

A viewing of the property held in advance of the auction. Pre-auction viewings are open to the public and may be attended at no charge.

Proxy bid

The auctioneers can undertake bidding on behalf of buyers unable to attend the auction in person. The buyers must contact the auction house prior to the auction to obtain an official, proxy bidding form. This must then be returned to the auction house with a deposit cheque within the time specified by the auctioneers. The buyer writes the maximum amount they will bid to on the form and the auctioneers will bid on behalf of the buyer, up to, but not beyond, the stated price.

Reserve

A reserve price is the lowest price the vendor will accept. This is agreed between the vendor and the Auctioneer. Most properties entered into the auction have a reserve price. This is confidential and not disclosed to any interested parties.

Telephone bid

A telephone bid, made by a member of staff from the auction house. The staff member telephones the client from the salesroom to bid on particular lots and relays the client's bids to the auctioneer during the bidding on those lots.

Tenancies

Contracts to occupy or lease the property subject to rent. A lot may be sold subject to existing tenancy agreements.

Withdrawal

Failure to reach the reserve price or insufficient bidding. The auctioneer will withdraw the property from the auction.

Index

General Structural Inspection, 45
Google maps, 4, 47
Ground rents, 11
Guide price, 3, 20, 96

Homebuyer Report, 44, 46
Houses in multiple occupation, 12

Industrial units, 13
investment properties, 11
Investment properties, 67

Legal documents, 3, 20
Legal pack, 28, 96
Local authority properties, 11

Memorandum of Sale, 21
Memorandum of sale., 77
Mixed Use Properties, 12
Mortgage, 28

Probates, 11
Proof of identity, 3, 19
Property Auction News, 33
Property insurance, 61
Property investors, 11
Property Misdescriptions Act 1991, 79
Property surveys, 41

Receivership sales, 11
Rental yields, 5, 66, 86, 91
Repossessions, 4, 10, 11, 35
Residential Investments, 12
Retail shops, 12, 13

Appendix 1 Directory of auction houses

Acuitus	t: 020 7034 4850 e: info@acuitus.co.uk	Acuitus 14 St Christopher's Place London W1U 1NH
Allsop (Commercial)	t: 020 7437 6977	Allsop (Commercial) 27 Soho Square London W1D 3AY
Allsop (Residential)	t: 020 7437 6977	Allsop (Residential) Moreau House 116 Brompton Road Knightsbridge London SW3 1JJ
Andrew Grant	t: 01905 616 101 e: commercial@andrew-grant.co.uk	Andrew Grant Commercial Department 5 Pierpoint Street Worcester WR1 1TA
Andrew Kelly	t: 01706 767 030 f: 01706 713432 e: auctions@andrew-kelly.co.uk	Andrew Kelly 124 Yorkshire Street Rochdale Lancashire OL16 1LA

Andrews & Robertson	t: 020 7808 8530 f: 020 7581 1973 e: auctions@a-r.co.uk	Andrews & Robertson 21-23 Mossop Street Chelsea London SW3 2LY
Arnolds	e: property@arnolds.uk.com t: 01603 620551	Arnolds 2 Prince of Wales Road Norwich Norolfk NR1 1LB
Ashby's Estate Agents	t: 01626 835845 e: homes@ashbys.uk.com	Ashby's Estate Agents Emlyn House Fore Street Bovey Tracey Devon TQ13 9AD
Astleys	t: 01792 479861 f: 01792 476926 e: sales@astleys.net	Astleys 49 Mansel Street Swansea SA1 5TB
Athawes	t: 020 8992 0056/0122 f: 020 8993 0511 e: mail@athawesauctioneers.co.uk	Athawes 203 High Street London W3 9DR
Auction House Atkinson & Keene	t: 01628 633376 f: 01628 770500	The Banking Hall 41 Queen Street Maidenhead SL6 1NB

Auction House Blundells	t: 0114 2230777 f: 0114 223 0760 e: blundells@auctionhouse.uk.net	Auction House Blundells 5 The Plaza 8 Fitzwilliam Street Sheffield S1 4JB
Auction House Coventry & Warwickshire	t: 01926 436131 e: newmans@auctionhouse.uk.net	Auction House Coventry & Warwickshire 8-9 Station Square Coventry CV1 2GT
Auction House Dee Atkinson & Harrison	t: 0845 4009900 f: 01377 241041 e: deeatkinsonharrison@auctionhouse.uk.net	Auction House Dee Atkinson & Harrison The Exchange Exchange Street Driffield YO25 6LD
Auction House Drewery and Wheeldon	t: 01427 616436 e: dreweryandwheeldon@auctionhouse.uk.net	Auction House Drewery and Wheeldon Rebrook House 124 Trinity Street Gainsborough DN21 1JD
Auction House East Kent Miles & Barr	t: 08445 738638 e: eastkent@auctionhouse.uk.net	Auction House East Kent Miles & Barr 51 Queen Street Ramsgate CT11 9EJ
Auction House Humphreys	t: 08444 180268 e: info@humphreysauctionhouse.co.uk	17-19 Lower Bridge Street Chester CH1 1RS

Auction House Lancashire (Farrell Heyworth)	t: 0845 3105700 e: lancashire@auctionhouse.uk.net	Auction House Lancashire (Farrell Heyworth) Second Floor Suite 309a Garstang Road Fulwood Preston PR2 4XJ
Auction House Newton Fallowell	t: 01476 591900 e: newtonfallowell@auctionhouse.uk.net	Auction House Newton Fallowell 68 High Street Grantham NG31 6NR
Auction House Norfolk & North Suffolk	t: 01603 505100 e: norwich@auctionhouse.uk.net	Auction House Norfolk & North Suffolk The Barn Newmarket Road Cringleford Norwich NR4 6UE
Auction House Smith and Sons	t: 0151 647 9272 f: 0151 649 0469 e: auctions@smithandsons.net.	Auction House Smith and Sons 51/52 Hamilton Square Birkenhead Wirral CH41 5BN
Auction House South Essex	t: 01268 695999 e: info@auctionhse.co.uk	Auction House South Essex 91 Furtherwick Road Canvey Island London SS8 7AY
Auction House South West	t: 01437 768677 f: 01437 768677	South West Wales FBM

Wales FBM	e: sales@fbmason-hwest.co.uk	6 Picton Place Haverfordwest Pembrokeshire SA61 2LX
Auction House Tees Valley	t: 08452 412112 e: teesvalley@auctionhouse.uk.net	Auction House Tees Valley 85 Borough Road Middlesbrough TS1 3AA
Auctions North East	t: 0191 383 2161 e: mail@auctionsnortheast.co.uk	Auctions North East 7 Old Elvet Durham City DH1 3HL
Auctions North West	t: 0161 653 4600 f: 0161 653 4601 e: info@auctionsnorthwest.co.uk	Auctions North West Birch Mill Business Centre Heywood Old Road Heywood OL10 2QQ
Austerberry	t: 01782 594595 f: 01782 594455 e: enquiries@austerberry.co.uk	Austerberry 4 Edensor Road Longton Stoke on Trent Staffordshire ST3 2NU
Austin Gray	t: 01273 201980 e: info@austingray.co.uk	Austin Gray 37 Vernon Terrace Brighton BN1 3JH
Baker Wynne and Wilson	t: 01270 625214 f: 01270 627627 e: enquiries@bakerwynneandwilson	Baker Wynne and Wilson 38 Pepper Street Nantwich Cheshire CW5 5AB

Barbers	t: 01743 276220 e: agricultural@barbers-online.co.uk	Finitor House Sitka Drive Shrewsbury Business Park Shrewsbury Shropshire SY2 6LG
Barnett Ross	e: enquiries@barnettross.co.uk	Barnett Ross Northway House 1379 High Road Whetstone London N20 9LP
Batcheller Thacker	t: 01892 512020 e: enquiries@batchellerthacker.co.uk	Batcheller Thacker No 1 London Road Tunbridge Wells Kent TN1 1DH
Baxtons	t: 0203 215 1015 f: 0207 920 9443 e: enquiries@lslps.co.uk	Baxtons 4th Floor 1-3 Sun Street London EC2A 2EP
Beesons	t: 01992 504020	Beesons 72 Railway Street Hertford SG14 1BQ
Bentons	t: 01664 563892 f: 01664 410223 e: sales@bentons.co.uk	Bentons 47 Nottingham Street Melton Mowbray Leicestershire LE13 1NN
Besley Hill	t: 0117 970 1551 f: 0117 970 1141 e: info@besleyhillsurveyit.co.uk	10 Badminton Road Downend Bristol BS16 6BQ

Bigwood	t: 0121 456 2200 e: auctions@bigwoodauctioneers.co.uk	Bigwood 51-52 Calthorpe Road Edgbaston Birmingham B15 1TH
Bill Jackson	t: 01432 344779	Bill Jackson 45 Bridge Street Hereford HR4 9DG
Bond Wolfe	t: 0121 525 0600 e: info@bondwolfe.net	Bond Wolfe West Plaza 8th Floor High Street West Bromwich B70 6JJ
Boot and Son	t: 01543 505454 e: info@bootandsonproperty.co.uk	Boot and Son 19 Wolverhampton Road Cannock Staffordshire WS11 1DG
Boultons	t: 01484 515029 e: sales@boultonsestateagents.co.uk	Boultons 54 John William Street Huddersfield West Yorkshire HD1 1ER
Bowen Son and Watson	t: 01691 622534 f: 01691 623603 e: ellesmere@bowensonandwatson.co.uk	Bowen Son and Watson Wharf Road Ellesmere Shropshire SY12 0EJ
Bradleys	e: richardpacey@beagroup.co.uk	Bradleys 16 Mannamead Road Plymouth Devon PL4 7AA

Bramleys	t: 01484 530361 e: auctions@bramleys1.co.uk	14 St. George's Square Huddersfield West Yorkshire HD1 1JF
Breach Wood Ingram	t: 01249 700737 e: enquiries@breachwoodingram.co.uk	Breach Wood Ingram The Estates Office Hartham Park Corsham Wiltshire SN13 0RP
Brendons Auctioneers	t: 08456 52 52 51 f: 020 8810 4862 e: auctioneers@brendons.co.uk	Brendons Auctioneers Royal Chambers 104 Pitshanger Lane London W5 1QX
Brights	t: 01237 473241 f: 01237 425215 e: mail@kevinbright.co.uk	Brights 18 Bridgeland Street Bideford Devon EX39 2QE
Brightwells	t: 01432 343800 e: property@brightwells.com	Brightwells Catherdral Chambers Broad Street Hereford HR4 9AS
Brown and Co (Residential)	t: 01603 629871 e: peter.hornor@brown-co.com	10 Queen Street City Centre Norwich NR2 4TA
Bruton Knowles	t: 0845 200 6489 e: enquiries@brutonknowles.co.uk	Bisley House Green Farm Business Park Bristol Road Gloucester GL2 4LY

Bullock & Lees	t: 01202 485187 e: post@bullockandlees.co.uk	4 Wick Lane Christchurch Dorset BH23 1HX
Bury and Hilton	t: 01782 575297 f: 01782 815485 e: burslemhomes@buryandhilton.co.uk	12 Moorland Road Burslem Stoke on Trent ST6 1DW
Butters John Bee	t: 01782 261511 e: headoffice@bjbmail.com	Butters John Bee Lakeview Festival Way Festival Park Stoke on Trent ST1 5BJ
Cavendish Ikin	t: 01244 404040 f: 01244 321246 e: auctions@cavendishikin.co.uk	Cavendish Ikin 2 Cuppin Street Chester Cheshire CH1 2BN
Charles Walker	t: 01274 814348 e: info@charles-walker.co.uk	Charles Walker Granby Barn 90 High Street Queensbury Bradford BD13 2PD
Charrison Properties	t: 020 8573 6120 e: info@charrisonproperties.co.uk	Charrison Properties 2nd Floor, Bridgewater House 866/868 Uxbridge Road Hayes Middlessex UB4 0RR
Cheffins	t: 01223 213777 e: property.auctions@cheffins.co.uk	Cheffins Clifton House 1 & 2 Clifton Road Cambridge CB1 7EA

Cheshire Property Auctions	t: 0151 547 1000 e: info@cpauctions.co.uk	Cheshire Property Auctions Suite 33 Admin Building Admin Road Knowsley L33 7TX
Chris Guttridge Auctioneers	t: 01709 872247 f: 01709 877397 e: enquiries@chrisguttridgeauctioneers.co.uk	Chris Guttridge Auctioneers 29-33 High Street Wath upon Dearne Rotherham S63 7QQ
Clarke and Simpson	t: 01728 621200 f: 01728 724667 e: email@clarkeandsimpson.co.uk	Clarke and Simpson Well Close Square Framlingham Suffolk IP13 9DU
Clarke Gammon Wellers	t: 01483 880905 f: 01483 880901 e: res.sales@clarkegammon.co.uk	Clarke Gammon Wellers 4 Quarry Street Guildford Surrey GU1 3TY
Clifford Dann	t: 01273 477022 e: lewes@clifforddann.co.uk	Clifford Dann Albion House Lewes East Sussex BN7 2NF
Clive Emson Auctioneers	t: 0845 8500333 e: auctions@cliveemson.co.uk	Clive Emson Auctioneers 8 Cavendish Way Bearstead Maidstone Kent ME15 8XY
	t: 0845 6036614	Clive Emson

Company	Contact	Address
Clive Emson Auctioneers	e: auctions@cliveemson.co.uk	Rostrum Lodge The Level Ditchling Road Brighton BN1 4SB
Clive Emson Auctioneers	t: 0845 6001265 e: auctions@cliveemson.co.uk	116 High Street Lee on the Solent Hampshire PO13 9DA
Codys	t: 01482 448 448 e: sales@codys.info	626 James Reckitt Avenue Hull HU8 0LG
Cooke and Arkwright	t: 01656 644 644 e: auctions@coark.com	One Central Park Western Avenue Bridgend CF31 3TZ
Cooper & Tanner	t: 01225 445167 e: countryhouse@cooperandtanner.co.uk	Cooper & Tanner 1 Harington Place Bath BA1 1HF
Copelands	t: 01246 232698 e: copelands.co@virgin.net	Copelands 5 Beetwell Street Chesterfield Derbyshire S40 1SH
Cottons	t: 0121 247 2233 e: auctions@cottons.co.uk	Cottons 361 Hagley Road Edgbaston Birmingham B17 8DL
Countrywide Property Auctions	t: 0870 2401140 e: office@auctions.cwea.co.uk	Countrywide Property Auctions 80-86 New London Road Chelmsford CM2 0PD
	t: 01454 321339	County Property

County Property		The Grange 73 Broad Street Chipping Sodbury South Gloucestershire BS37 6AD
Cushman & Wakefield	t: 020 7152 5025	Cushman & Wakefield 43-45 Portman Square London W1A 3BG
D J Keys	t: 01803 214 214 e: property@djkeys.co.uk	D J Keys 121 Union Street Torquay Devon TQ1 3DW
Darlows	t: 0845 6732168 e: auctions@darlows.co.uk	Darlows Wellington House Butt Road Colchester Essex CO3 3DA
Dawsons Estate Agents	t: 01792 643974 e: sw@dawsonsproperty.co.uk	Dawsons Estate Agents 11 Walter Road Swansea SA1 5NF
Dedman Gray	t: 01702 311111 f: 01702 587970 e: commercial@dedmangray.co.uk	Dedman Gray 103 The Broadway Thorpe Bay Essex SS1 3HQ
Denton Clark and Co	t: 01244 409 660 f: 01244 315 954 e: enquiries@dentonclark.co.uk	Denton Clark and Co 4 Vicars Lane Chester CI I1 1QU

Dodds Property World	t: 01352 752552 e: dodds@door-key.com	9 Chester Street Mold Flintshire CH7 1EG
Dreweat Neatte	t: 01672 514916 e: marlborough@dreweatt-neate.co.uk	93 High Street Marlborough Wiltshire SN8 1HD
Drewery & Wheeldon	t: 01427 616118 e: info@dreweryandwheeldon.co.uk	Drewery & Wheeldon Rebrook House 124 Trinity Street Gainsborough Lincolnshire DN21 1JD
Drivers Norris	t: 020 7607 5001 e: auction@drivers.co.uk	Drivers Norris 407/409 Holloway Road London N7 6HP
Durrants	t: 01502 470423 e: rebecca.mayhew@durrants.com	Durrants 10 New Market Beccles Suffolk NR34 9HA
Eddisons	t: 0113 2430101 e: leedsauctions@eddisons.com	Eddisons Pennine House Russell Street Leeds LS1 5RN
Eddisons	t: 0161 831 9444 e: manchesterauctions@eddisons.com	Eddisons Bow Chambers 8 Tib Lane Manchester M2 4JB
Edward Mellor Auctions	t: 0161 443 4740 e: auction@edwardmellor.co.uk	Edward Mellor Auctions Number One St Petersgate Stockport SK1 !EB

Edwards Moore Estate Agents	t: 01922 615 222 e: wallsales@edwardsmoore.co.uk	Edwards Moore Estate Agents Estate House Darwell Street Walsall WS1 1DA
Elder and Twells	t: 01773 535353 f: 01773 531990 e: heanor@elderandtwells.co.uk	Elder and Twells 15 Market Street Heanor Derbyshire DE75 7NR
Eleys Auctions	t: 01205 316600 e: auctions@eleys.co.uk	Eleys Auctions Haven Business Park Boston PE21 7AA
Elliott Auctions	t: 01923 212112 e: elliott@watford27.fsnet.co.uk	Elliott Auctions 133 The Parade Watford Hertfordshire WD17 1NA
Erinaceous Auctions (Commercial)	t: 0207808 3434 e: commercial@erinaceous.com	Erinaceous Auctions (Commercial) 34 St James's Street London SW1A 1HD
Erinaceous Auctions (Residential)	t: 0870 703 9090 e: residential@erinaceous.com	Erinaceous Auctions (Residential) Saffron House Saffron Hill London EC1N 8YB
Fairfax & Co	t: 01446 771777 e: allan@fairfaxandco.co.uk	Fairfax & Co 75 High Street Cowbridge Vale of Glamorgan CF71 7AF

Farrell Heyworth	t: 0845 3105700 e: auctions@farrellheyworth.co.uk	Farrell Heyworth Auction Department 8 Poulton Street Kirkham PR4 2AB
Feather Smailes and Scales	t: 01423 501211 f: 01423 500215 e: info@fss4property.co.uk	Feather Smailes and Scales 8 Raglan St Harrogate North Yorkshire HG1 1LE
Fidler Taylor and Co	t: 01629 580228 f: 01629 580235 e: matlock@fidler-taylor.co.uk	Fidler Taylor and Co Crown Square Matlock DE4 3AT
Fisher German	t: 01530 412821 e: ashby@fishergerman.co.uk	Fisher German The Grange 80 Tamworth Road Ashby de la Zouch LE65 2BY
Fisher Wrathwall	t: 01524 68822 e: property@fisherwrathall.co.uk	Fisher Wrathwall The Old Warehouse Castle Hill Lancaster LA1 1YP
Fox Grant	t: 0870 745 600 e: admin@foxgrant.com	Fox Grant Fox Barn Lower Woodford Salisbury SP4 6NQ
Fry & Co	t: 0800 195 0044 e: enquiries@fryandco.com	Fry & Co Bowen House Bredgar Road Gillingham Kent ME9 7PW

116

Company	Contact	Address
Fulfords	t: 0870 241 4343 e: info@westcountrypropertyauctions.co.uk	Fulfords Auction Department 44 Rolle Street Exmouth Devon EX8 2SH
Future Property Auctions	t: 0141-632-6599 e: info@futurepropertyauctions.co.uk	Future Property Auctions 196 Kilmarnock Road Glasgow Scotland G41 3PG
G Herbert Banks	t: 01299 896968 f: 01299 896981	G Herbert Banks The Estate Office Hill House Great Witley Worcester WR6 6JB
Gascoigne Halman	t: 01625 536434 e: wilmslow@gascoignehalman.co.uk	52 Alderley Road Wilmslow SK9 1NY
George F White	t: 01665 603231 f: 01665 510872	George F White 6 Market Street Alnwick Northumberland NE66 1TL
Goadsby	t: 01202 673375 e: jim.doerr@goadsby.com	Goadsby 245 High Street North Poole Dorset BH15 1DX
Goldings	t: 01473 210200 e: info@goldingsauctions.co.uk	Goldings 9 St Helens Street Ipswich Suffolk IP4 1HE

Graham Penny Auctions	t: 01332 242880	3-5 St James's Street Derby DE1 1QT
Graham Watkins	t: 01538 373308 f: 01538 399653 e: info@grahamwatkins.co.uk	69 Derby Street Leek Staffordshire ST13 6JL
Greenslade Taylor Hunt	t: 01823 277121 e: residential.taunton@gth.net	Greenslade Taylor Hunt 13 Hammet Street Taunton Somerset TA1 1RN
Griffin Property Auctioneers	t: 01268 567777 e: steve.healey@griffinresidential.co.uk	Griffin Property Auctioneers 30 Southernhay Basildon Essex SS14 1EL
Griffiths & Charles	t: 01905 726464 e: info@griffiths-charles.co.uk	Griffiths & Charles 57 Foregate Street Worcester WR1 1DZ
Gwilym Richards and Co	t: 01600 860 300 f: 01600 861 933 e: info@grichards.co.uk	Gwilym Richards and Co The Estate Office Pant Glas Llanishen Chepstow Monmouthshire NP16 6QQ
Hair and Son Ltd	t: 01702 432255 f: 01702 337846 e: auction@haircommercial.co.uk	Hair and Son Ltd 200 London Road Southend-on-Sea Essex SS1 1PJ

Halls Estate Agents	t: 01743 284777 e: welshbridge@halls.to	Halls Estate Agents Welsh Bridge 1 Frankwell Shrewsbury Shropshire SY3 8LA
Handley Gibson Twaites	t: 0113 243 3961 e: karen@handleygibsontwaites.co.uk	Handley Gibson Twaites 3 Oxford Place Leeds LS1 3AX
Harman Healy	t: 020 8649 7255 f: 020 8666 0559 e: residential@harman-healy.co.uk	Harman Healy 23 Brighton Road South Croydon Surrey CR2 6EA
Harrison Coward Estate Agents	t: 01229 582056 e: info@harrison-coward.co.uk	County Square Ulveston Cumbria LA12 7AB
Harry Ray & Company	t: 01938 552 555 f: 01938 554 678 e: info@harryray.com	Harry Ray & Company 37 Broad Street Welshpool Powys SY21 7RR
Hawkesford	t: 01926 430553 f: 01926 430538 e: leamington@hawkesford.co.uk	Hawkesford 6 Euston Place Leamington CV32 4LN
HEB	t: 0115 950 6611 f: 0115 950 6622 e: info@heb.co.uk	HEB 17 The Ropewalk Nottingham NG1 5DU
Herbert R Thomas	t: 01446 772911 e: property@hrt.uk.com	Herbert R Thomas 59 High Street Cowbridge CF71 7YL

Name	Contact	Address
Hobbs Parker Estate Agents	t: 01233 502222 e: estateagents@hobbsparker.co.uk	Romney House Monument Way Orbital Park Ashford Kent TN24 0HB
Hollier Browne	t: 0121 458 7421	1880 Pershore Road Kings Norton Birmingham B30 3AS
Hough & Co	t: 01543 414126 f: 01543 414761	22 Market Street Lichfield Staffordshire WS13 6LH
Howkins and Harrison	t: 01788 564680 f: 01788 540257 e: rugrural@howkinsandharrison.co.uk	7-11 Albert Street Rugby Warwickshire CV21 2RX
Humberts	t: 01451 830383 e: stow@humberts.co.uk	Humberts The Square Stow on the Wold Cheltenham GL54 1BL
Hunters	t: 01904 756116 e: auctions@huntersnet.co.uk	Hunters 18/19 Colliergate York YO1 8BN
Husseys	t: 01392 250441 e: property@husseys.co.uk	Husseys Property Office Alphin Brook Road Exeter EX2 8TH
J H Walter	t: 01522 504360 e: info@jhwalter.co.uk	J H Walter 1 Mint Lane Lincoln LN1 1UD

.Straker Chadwick and Sons	t: 01873 852624 f: 01873 857311 e: info@strakerchadwick.com	J.Straker Chadwick and Sons Market Street Chambers Abergavenny Monmouthshire NP7 5SD
JH Walter	t: 01522 504360 e: info@jhwalter.co.uk	JH Walter 1 Mint Lane Lincoln LN1 1UD
John Amos and Co	t: 01568 610310 f: 01568 620002 e: property@johnamos.co.uk	John Amos and Co 2 Broad Street Leominster Herefordshire HR6 8BS.
John Earle	t: 01564 79 43 43 f: 01564 79 49 57 e: peter.c@johnearle.co.uk	John Earle 74 High Street Henley-in-Arden Warwickshire B95 5BX
John Francis	t: 01267 233111 e: carmarthen@johnfrancis.co.uk	John Francis 18 Lammas Street Carmarthen SA31 3AJ
John German	t: 01283 512244 e: burton@johngerman.co.uk	John German 1 Lichfield Street Burton Upon Trent Staffordshire DE14 3QZ
John Goodwin	t: 01531 633729 e: ledbury@johngoodwin.co.uk	3-5 New Street Ledbury HR8 2DX
John Sanders	t: 01527 575525 e: bromsgrove@john-sanders.co.uk	John Sanders 8 New Road Bromsgrove Worcestershire B60 2JD

John Woollett & Co	t: 01908 222020 f: 01908 221553 e: johnwoollett@btconnect.com	3 Radcliffe Street Wolverton Milton Keynes MK12 5DQ
Jones Lang Lasalle	t: 020 7821 8888	1 Warwick Row London SW1E 5ER
Jones Peckover	t: 01745 812127 f: 01745 816429 e: denbigh@jonespeckover.com	47 Vale St Denbigh Clwyd
Keane Mahony Smith	t: 021 427 0311 f: 021 427 1296 e: cork@k-m-s.com	Keane Mahony Smith 44 South Mall Cork Ireland
Keys	t: 01603 629158 e: norwich@gakey.co.uk	Keys 13 Upper King Street Norwich NR3 1RB
King Sturge	t: 020 7493 4933 f: 020 7087 5555 e: contactus@kingsturge.com	King Sturge London West End 30 Warwick Street London W1B 5NH
Kivells	t: 01237 472146 e: bideford@kivells.com	Kivells 4 Bridgeland Street Bideford Devon EX39 2PS
Lambert and Foster	t: 01892 832 325 f: 01892 834 700 e: auctions@lambertandfoster.co.uk	Lambert and Foster Paddock Wood Office 77 Commercial Road Paddock Wood Kent TN12 6DS

Langleys	t: 020 8298 1707	Langley House 249 Broadway Bexleyheath Kent DA6 8DB
Leonards	t: 01482 375212 e: info@leonards-hull.co.uk	512 Holderness Road Hull East Yorkshire HU9 2DS
Lodge and Thomas	t: 01872 27 27 22 f: 01872 22 36 65 e: auctions@lodgeandthomas.co.uk	58 Lemon Street Truro Cornwall TR1 2PY
Louis Johnson	t: 01670 513025 e: ljestates@btconnect.com	Louis Johnson Oswald House 63 Bridge Street Morpeth Northumberland NE61 1PQ
Loveitts	t: 024 7652 7789 e: coventry.residential@loveitts.co.uk	Loveitts 29 Warwick Row Coventry Warwickshire CV1 1DY
Luscombe Maye	t: 01548 830831 e: andrea.hack@luscombemaye.com	Luscombe Maye 3 Church Street Modbury PL21 0QW
Maggs and Allen	t: 0117 949 1888 f: 0117 949 2000 e: admin@maggsandallen.co.uk	Maggs and Allen 60A Northumbria Drive Henleaze Bristol BS9 4HW
Main and Main	t: 0161 437 5337 f: 0161 499 0035 e: martinM@mainandmain.co.uk	Main and Main 1st Floor 198 Finney Lane Heald Green Cheshire SK8 3QA

Manning Stainton
t: 0113 393 3482
e: auctionhouse@manningstainton.co.uk
12 Feast Field
Horsforth
Leeds
LS18 4TJ

Mark Jenkinson & son
t: 0114 276 0151
f: 0114 275 2570
8 Norfolk Row
Sheffield
S1 2PA

Marshs Auctioneers
t: 021 4270347
e: info@marshsauctioneers.ie
Marshs Auctioneers
17 South Mall
Cork
County Cork
Ireland

Martin and Pole
t: 0118 979 0460
f: 0118 977 6166
e: a@martinpole.co.uk
Martin and Pole
10 Milton Road
Wokingham
Berkshire
RG40 1DB

McCartneys
t: 01588 672385
e: cravenarms@mccartneys.co.uk
McCartneys
Corvedale Road
Craven Arms
Shropshire
SY7 9NE

McHugh and Co
t: 020 7485 0112
f: 020 7485 3128
e: james@mchughandcompany.co.uk
McHugh and Co
71 Parkway
Regents Park
London
NW1 7PP

Mellor Braggins
t: 01565 632618
f: 01565 755679
e: surveys.knutsford@mellerbraggins.com
Mellor Braggins
Head Office
35/37 Princess Street
Knutsford
WA16 6BP

Merseyside Property Auctions (MPA)
t: 0151 260 9873
f: 0151 260 9779
e: k.hughes@mpalimited.co.uk
Merseyside Property Auctions (MPA)
Number 5
Prescot Street
Liverpool
L7 8UE

Metcalfs	t: 01253 624047 f: 01253 624978 e: sales@metcalfestateagents.co.uk	73 Topping Street Blackpool Lancashire FY1 3AF
Michael C.L. Hodgson	t: 01539 721375 e: enquiries@michael-cl-hodgson.co.uk	36 Finkle Street Kendal LA9 4AB
Michael Poole	t: 01642 254222 f: 01642 743 444 e: mike.poole@michaelpoole.co.uk	Michael Poole 64 - 66 Borough Road Middlesbrough TS1 2JH
Michelmore Hughes	t: 01803 862002 e: sales@michelmorehughes.co.uk	Michelmore Hughes The Old Surgery 26 Fore Street Totnes TQ9 5DX
Miller and Son	t: 01872 277794 f: 01872 242085 e: comprigney@millerson.com	Miller and Son Comprigney Comprigney Hill Truro Cornwall TR1 3EF
Miller Metcalf	t: 08445 796633 e: auction@mmauction.co.uk	Miller Metcalf 11 Institute Street Bolton BL1 1PZ
Moore Allen and Innocent	t: 01285 648105 f: 01285 640494 e: surveyors@mooreallen.co.uk	Moore Allen and Innocent 33 Castle Street Cirencester Gloucestershire GL7 1QD
Morgan Bedoe	t: 0117 9464949 e: post@morgan-beddoe.co.uk	Morgan Bedoe 147 Whiteladies Road Clifton Bristol BS8 2QT

Mullucks Wells	t: 01371 872117 e: ttrembath@mullucks.co.uk	Mullucks Wells The Old Town Hall Great Dunmow Essex CM6 1AU
MustbeSold.com	t: 0207 4071743	MustbeSold.com 35-37 Chaseside Southgate London N14 5BP
Nesbits	t: 023 9286 4321 f: 023 9229 5522 e: davidnesbit@nesbits.co.uk	Nesbits 7 Clarendon Road Southsea PO5 2ED
Newland Rennie Wilkins	t: 01633 221441 e: newport@nrwproperty.com	Newland Rennie Wilkins 68 Bridge Street Newport South Wales NP20 4AQ
North West Property Auctions	t: 01925 490711 e: info@northwestpropertyauctions.com	North West Property Auctions 98 Carrington Close Birchwood Warrington WA3 7QB
Osborne King	t: 028 9027 0000 e: property@osborneking.com	Osborne King The Metro Building 6-9 Donegall Square South Belfast BT1 5JA
Palmer Auctioneers	t: +353 051 872061 f: +353 051 87206	Palmer Auctioneers 2/3 Colbeck Street Waterford City

Parrys Property	t: 01873 858990 e: abergavenny@parrysproperty.co.uk	17 Nevill Street Abergavenny Monmouthshire NP7 5AA
Parsons Son and Basley	t: 01273 326171 f: 01273 821224 e: property@psandb.co.uk	32 Queens Road Brighton BN1 3YE
Pattinson	t: 0845 1461582 f: 0191 4960139 e: auctions@pattinson.co.uk	Pattinson 4 Fellside Road Whickham Newcastle Upon Tyne NE16 4JU
Paul Fosh Auctions	t: 01633 254044 e: info@paulfoshauctions.co.uk	Paul Fosh Auctions 87 Church Road Newport NP19 7EH
Paul Jackson	t: 01590 674411 e: enquiries@pauljackson.co.uk	Paul Jackson The Yacht House The Quay Lymington Hants SO41 3AS
Pennine Ways	t: 01434 381808 e: info@countrycottages.net	Pennine Ways Market House Market Place Alston Cumbria CA9 3HS
Penny Cuick Collins	t: 0121 665 4150 e: info@pennycuick.co.uk	Penny Cuick Collins 9 The Square 111 Broad Street Birmingham B15 1AS
Penrith Farmers' and Kidd's	t: 01768 890781 f: 01768 895058 e: info@pfkauctions.co.uk	Skirsgill Saleroom Skirsgill Penrith CA11 0DN

Perkins George Mawer & Co	t: 01673 843011 e: info@perkinsgeorgemawer.co.uk	Corn Exchange Chambers Queen Street Market Rasen Lincolnshire LN8 3EH
Peter Alan Estate Agents	t: 0800 905 905	Ty Croes Cwrlwys Copthorne Way Park Valegate Retail Park Culverhouse Cross Cardiff CF5 6EH
Phillips Smith and Dunn	t: 01237 423007 f: 01237 423023 e: Bideford@phillipsland.com	31 Bridgeland Street Bideford Devon EX39 2PS
Pugh & Company	t: 0844 2 722444 f: 0844 2 722555 e: admin@pugh-auctions.com	Pugh & Company 4 The Parks Newton le Willows WA12 0JQ
R G & R B Williams	t: 01989 567233 f: 01989 567260 e: info@rgandrbwilliams.co.uk	R G & R B Williams Windsor House St May's Street Ross-on-Wye Herefordshire HR9 5HT
Reeman Dansie Auctions	t: 01206 754754 e: auctions@reemans.com	Reeman Dansie Auctions Unit 8 Wyncolls Road Severalls Business Park Colchester CO4 9HT

Rendells	t: 01626 353881 e: newtonabbot@rendells.co.uk	Rendells 13 Market Street Newton Abbot South Devon TQ12 2RL
Richard Turner and Son	t: 01200 441351 f: 01200 441666 e: property@rturner.co.uk	Richard Turner and Son Old Sawley Grange Sawley, Near Clitheroe BB74LH
Robert Ellis	t: 0115 946 1818 e: longeaton@robertellis.co.uk	Robert Ellis 50 Market Place Long Eaton Nottingham NG10 1LT
Robertson Smith and Kempson	t: 020 8840 7677 e: commercial@rskproperty.co.uk	Robertson Smith and Kempson 15 The Mall Ealing London W5 2PJ
Robin Jessop	t: 01677 425950 f: 01677 426059 e: info@robinjessop.co.uk	Robin Jessop North End Bedale North Yorkshire DL8 1AB
Robinson and Hall	t: 01473 831531 f: 01473 832200 e: ipswich@robinsonandhall.co.uk	Robinson and Hall Broomvale Business Centre Little Blakenham Ipswich IP8 4JU
Romans	t: 0118 9366 688 e: auctions@romans.co.uk	Romans Hatch Farm Mill Lane Sindlesham Wokingham Berkshire RG41 5DF

Sale No Fee	t: 07795 478243 f: 01352 752215 e: enquiries@forallsurveys.co.uk	Sale No Fee Survey Department 16-18 Chester Street Mold Flintshire CH7 1EG
Salter McGuinness	t: 0208 907 1222 e: homes@saltermcguinness.co.uk	Cornwall House 325 Kenton Road Kenton Harrow Middlesex HA3 0XN
Savills (Commercial)	t: 020 7877 4514	20 Grosvenor Hill Berkley Square London W1K 3HQ
Savills (Nottingham)	t: 0115 934 8020	9 Fletcher Gate Nottingham NG1 1QQ
Savills (Residential)	t: 020 7824 9091	Savills (Residential) 139 Sloane Street London SW1X 9AY
Scargill Mann and Co	t: 01332 207720 f: 01332 207710 e: enquiries@scargillmann.co.uk	Scargill Mann and Co 4 St. James's Street Derby DE1 1RL
Screetons	t: 01430 431201 e: howden@screetons.co.uk	Screetons 25 Bridgegate Howden East Riding of Yorkshire DN14 7AA

Seel and Co	t: 029 2037 0117 f: 029 2037 0121 e: info@rhseel.co.uk	Seel and Co The Crown House Wyndham Crescent Canton Cardiff CF11 9UH
Seldons	t: 01237 477997 e: estateagents@seldons.co.uk	Seldons 15 The Quay Bideford Devon EX39 2EZ
Sharpes	t: 01274 731217 f: 01274 370850	Sharpes 4 Upper Piccadilly Bradford West Yorkshire BD1 3PQ
Shobrook & Co Ltd.	t: 01752 255157 e: info@shobrook.co.uk	Shobrook & Co Ltd. 20 Western Approach Plymouth PL1 1TG
Shonki Brothers	t: 0116 254 3373 e: info@shonkibrothers.com	Shonki Brothers 55 London Road Leicester LE2 OPE
Shortland Horne	t: 024 7655 9007 e: commercial@shortland-horne.co.uk	Shortland Horne Warwick Gate 21/22 Warwick Row Coventry CV1 1ET
SHP	t: 01772 555403 e: info@shpvaluersltd.co.uk	SHP 69 Garstang Road Preston Lancashire PR1 1LB

Shuldham Calverley	t: 01777 709943 e: rescom@shuldham-calverley.co.uk	Shuldham Calverley 21 Exchange Street Retford Nottinghamshire DN22 6BL
Silverwoods	t: 01200 423325 e: info@silverwoods.co.uk	Silverwoods Clitheroe Auction Mart Ribblesdale Centre Lincoln Way Clitheroe Lancashire BB7 1QD
Smith and Sons	t: 0151 647 9272 f: 0151 649 0469 e: aas@smithandsons.net	Smith and Sons 51/52 Hamilton Square Birkenhead Wirral CH41 5BN
Stags	t: 01392 426183 e: exeter@stags.co.uk	Stags 21 Southernhay West Exeter Devon EX1 1PR
Stephen & Co	t: 01934 621101 e: post@stephenand.co.uk	Stephen & Co Central Chambers Walliscote Road Weston Super Mare Somerset BS23 1UP
Strakers	t: 01380 727105 e: auctions@strakers.co.uk	Strakers 9 St.John Street Devizes Wiltshire SN10 1BD
Stratton and	t: 01392 278466	Stratton and

Holborow's	f: 01392 412467 e: exeter@stratton-holborow.co.uk	8 Southernhay West Exeter Devon EX1 1JG
Strettons	t: 020 8520 8383 e: auctions@strettons.co.uk	Central House 189-203 Hoe Street London E17 3SZ
Suffolks.co.uk	t: 01473 210200 e: info@suffolks.co.uk	St Margarets Street Ipswich Suffolk IP4 2AX
Sullivan Mitchell	t: 0208 944 8899 e: sullivanmitchell@btconnect.com	404-406 Garratt Lane Earlsfield London SW18 4HP
Sullivan Mitchell	t: 0844 800 6884 e: lymington@sullivanmitchell.co.uk	36 St Thomas Street Lymington Hampshire SO41 9NE
Sunderlands & Thompsons	t: 01432 356161 f: 01432 352956 e: enquiries@st-hereford.co.uk	Sunderlands & Thompsons Offa House St Peters Square Hereford HR1 2PQ
Sutton Kersh	t: 0870 873 1212 e: auctions@suttonkersh.co.uk	Sutton Kersh 2 Cotton Street Liverpool L3 7DY
Sutton Kersh Binstock	t: 0208 449 5599 f: 0208 449 5493 e: info@skbauctions.co.uk	Sutton Kersh Binstock Albany House 10 Wood Street Barnet Hertfordshire EN5 4BW

Company	Contact	Address
SVA	e: info@sva-auctions.co.uk	13 Great King Street Edinburgh EH3 6QW
Symonds and Sampson	t: 01258 473766 f: 01258 472540	Agriculture House Market Place Sturminster Newton Dorset DT10 1AR
Taylor Underwood	t: 01271 323 290 e: info@tuprop.co.uk	Taylor Underwood 102 Boutport Street Barnstaple Devon EX31 1SY
The Country Property Agents	t: 01454 321339 e: enquiries@countryproperty.co.uk	The Country Property Agents The Grange 73 Broad Street Chipping Sodbury South Gloucestershire BS37 6ND
The Property People	t: 0845 0871111 e: auctions@tppuk.com	The Property People North Wales Auction House 23 Church Street Llangefni Anglesey LL77 7DU
Thompson Wilson	t: 01494 474234 e: auctions@thompsonwilson.co.uk	Thompson Wilson 1 Amersham Hill High Wycombe Buckinghamshire HP13 6NQ

Tom Spillane and Co. Ltd	t: +353 064 6633066 f: +353 064 663395	5 Kenmare Place Killarney Co.Kerry
Tops	t: 01603 750450	Tops Auction House 15-17 Princes Street Norwich NR3 1AF
Tudor Network Auctions	t: 01702 346818 f: 01702 430955	Tudor Network Auctions Swan Hall 255 - 261 Victoria Avenue Southend on Sea Essex SS2 6NE
TW Glaze	t: 01379 641 341 f: 01379 651 936 e: prop@twgaze.co.uk	TW Glaze 10 Market Hill Diss Norfolk IP22 4WJ
Venmore Thomas and Jones	t: 0151 236 6746 f: 0151 227 3407	Venmore Thomas and Jones 8-10 Stanley Street Liverpool L1 6AF
W M Sykes	t: 01484 683543 e: info@wmsykes.co.uk	W M Sykes 38 Huddersfield Road Holmfirth Huddersfield HD9 3JH
W.A. Barnes	t: 01623 554084 f: 01623 550764 e: sales@wabarnes.co.uk	W.A. Barnes Portland Square Sutton in Ashfield Nottinghamshire NG17 1DA

Name	Contact	Address
Ward and Partners	t: 01634 735630 f: 01634 735631 e: auction@wardandpartners.co.uk	Ward and Partners Christchurch House, Beaufort Court Sir Thomas Longley Road Medway City Estate Rochester Kent ME2 4FX
Webbers Commercial	t: 01271 347888 e: commercial@webbers.co.uk	Webbers Commercial 4 Queen Street Barnstaple EX32 8HG
Westcountry Property Auctions	t: 0870 241 4343 e: info@westcountrypropertyauctions.co.uk	Westcountry Property Auctions 44 Rolle Street Exmouth Devon EX8 2SH
Whitegates	t: 0151 523 0800	Liverpool Merseyside L9 2BU
Whittaker and Biggs	t: 01260 279858 f: 01260 291053 e: allan.pickering@whittakerandbiggs.co.uk	Whittaker and Biggs Brown Street Congleton Cheshire CW12 1QY.
William H Brown Property Auctions - Leeds	t: 01302 710490 f: 01302 710854 e: leedsauctions@sequencehome.co.uk	William H Brown Property Auctions - Leeds 38 High Street Bawtry Doncaster South Yorkshire DN10 6JE

Willmotts	t: 020 8222 9901	Willmotts Willmott House 12 Blacks Road Hammersmith London W6 9EU
Willsons Chartered Surveyors	t: 01507 463582 f: 01507 462422 e: alford@willsons-property.co.uk	Willsons Chartered Surveyors 124 West Street Alford Lincs LN13 9DR
Wilsons Auctions	t: 02890 342626 e: mallusk@wilsonauctions.com	Wilsons Auctions Mallusk Road Newtownabbey Co Antrim Northern Ireland BT36 4PP
Wilsons Auctions	t: 01294 833444 e: scotland@wilsonsauctions.com	Wilsons Auctions 6 Kilwinning Road Dalry Ayrshire Scotland KA24 4LG
Wilsons Auctions	t: +353 4642800 e: dublin@wilsonsauctions.com	Wilsons Auctions Kingswood Cross Naas Road Dublin 22 Ireland
Zoopla (REDC)	e: auctionsupport@zoopla.co.uk	Zoopla (REDC) 0844 858 4074

•

www.straightforwardco.co.uk

All titles, listed below, in the Straightforward Guides Series can be purchased online, using credit card or other forms of payment by going to www.straightfowardco.co.uk A discount of 25% per title is offered with online purchases.

Law
A Straightforward Guide to:

Consumer Rights
Bankruptcy Insolvency and the Law
Employment Law
Private Tenants Rights
Family law
Business law
Public law
Small Claims in the County Court
Contract law
Intellectual Property and the law
Divorce and the law
Leaseholders Rights
The Process of Conveyancing
Knowing Your Rights and Using the Courts
Producing Your own Will
Housing Rights
The Bailiff the law and You
Probate and The Law
Company law
What to Expect When You Go to Court
Guide to Competition Law
Give me Your Money-Guide to Effective Debt Collection
Caring for a Disabled Child

General titles
Letting Property for Profit
Buying, Selling and Renting property
Buying a Home in England and France
Bookkeeping and Accounts for Small Business
Creative Writing
Freelance Writing
Writing Your own Life Story
Writing performance Poetry
Writing Romantic Fiction
Speech Writing
Teaching Your Child to Read and write
Teaching Your Child to Swim
Raising a Child-The Early Years
Creating a Successful Commercial Website
The Straightforward Business Plan
The Straightforward C.V.
Successful Public Speaking
Handling Bereavement
Play the Game-A Compendium of Rules
Individual and Personal Finance
Understanding Mental Illness
The Two Minute Message
Guide to Self Defence
Buying a Used Car
Tiling for Beginners
Starting your Own Online Business
Buying and Selling on Online Auction Sites

Go to:

www.straightforwardco.co.uk